CONCILIUM

Religion in the Eighties

CONCILIUM

Editorial Directors

Concilium 169 (9/1983): Spirituality

JOB
AND THE
SILENCE OF GOD

Edited by
Christian Duquoc
and
Casiano Floristán

English Language Editor
Marcus Lefébure

T. & T. CLARK LTD
Edinburgh

THE SEABURY PRESS
New York

November 1983
T. & T. Clark Ltd, 36 George Street, Edinburgh EH2 2LQ
ISBN: 0 567 30049 8

The Seabury Press, 815 Second Avenue, New York, NY 10017
ISBN: 0 8164 2449 7

Library of Congress Catalog Card No.: 82 062762

Printed in Scotland by William Blackwood & Sons Ltd, Edinburgh

Concilium: Monthly except July and August. ISSN: 0010-5236.
Subscriptions 1983: UK and Rest of the World £27·50, postage and handling included (new subscribers £25·00); USA and Canada, all applications for subscriptions and enquiries about *Concilium* should be addressed to The Seabury Press, 815 Second Avenue, New York, NY 10017, USA.

CONTENTS

Editorial

THE BOOK of Job is a fire-ball. It destroys the neat arrangement devised by some adherents of the religion of Israel to reject painful questions. It disturbs the harmony of biblical teaching about God's plan; it makes room for chance, for the irrational. It refuses to soften what everyone seeks to control, suffering and misfortune. It opposes the clarity of a moral order as the law of history.

To choose to meditate on this book in our age is therefore not without significance. Many Christians are tempted to regard it as a book testifying to a crisis in the religion of Israel, and their judgment is not incorrect. Roderick MacKenzie's article, which places the book in its cultural and historical background, does justice to this view. But a book of the Bible is an element in the Book: it is not a bygone moment, but as present for us as the totality of the biblical writings. It would not have its present place in community worship if it were deemed to be an archaeological document. And yet its current application is not straightforward, since the book is so charged with human drama; Fr Philippe Rouillard's essay shows the liturgy's hesitation over it.

Application to the present requires, first, respect for the text, an effort to listen to it with the help of the instruments which can enable us to measure its distance from us and to grasp its present power. Claus Westermann helps us here by explaining the ambiguity of Job in terms of the literary form of the work. François Chirpaz takes us into the heart of the debate about the figure of Job's God by analysing the modern, Marxist, atheist interpretation of Ernst Bloch. Job revolts against God and submits to him; he does not deny him. He opens the way towards a more complex relation than that embodied in the dichotomy of a dominating God and a subject man versus a non-existent God and free man.

This greater complexity is represented in the ambiguity of the figure of God and in the disturbing representation of Satan. Dirk Kinet has undertaken to explore this structural feature which explains Job's battle. Job's battle is against the defenders of the clarity of God's ways, his friends, who come to console him and in fact burden him. Are the friends completely wrong? Do they not represent, in the face of Job's exaggerated accusations, an important element in the trial? Jean Lévêque thinks so, and explains his view in the article entitled 'Tradition and Betrayal in the Speeches of the Friends'.

So what do Job and his friends hope for in this trial which sets them against each other? A reply from God. Job's God is not silent; he speaks. He delivers a strange speech. Its meaning is made the more obscure because it is cast in an ironic vein; Luis Alonso-Schökel gives us an interpretation.

This interpretation cannot be separated from the judgment to be made of another case of an innocent victim abandoned and suffering, Jesus. The book of Job is an element in the Book, and for the Christian the Book includes the gospels. What relation is there between the passion of Job and that of Jesus? Jean-Claude Sagne has attempted to throw light on this question, and to prevent the cross of Christ from draining Job's revolt of meaning.

Present application cannot simply stick to the text; it has to bring out the symbolic connotations it may evoke. Three articles are devoted to these resonances in the present. One is on the political level: Enrique Dussel uses Job to decode the passion of the people of El Salvador. Another investigates, through the work of a modern film director, Bergmann, the effects of this question from the depths of history, while the last studies its echoes in history.

This work from afar shakes us by its vehemence. One of us completes the process of listening to it by showing that this quality of unexpectedness in God, that is, our inability to confine him to the realm of morality, is in the Bible the key to his complicity with our revolt against the fate reserved for human beings.

CHRISTIAN DUQUOC
CASIANO FLORISTÁN

PART I

The Situation

Roderick MacKenzie

The Cultural and Religious Background of the Book of Job

1. THE DATE OF COMPOSITION

TO ATTEMPT to situate the Book of Job in its proper time and space is an enterprise bordering on the foolhardy. As regards date, almost every period from the time of Moses to the Hellenistic age has been proposed by one authority or another as its birthdate. The choice is more limited as regards geographical location, yet even for that we cannot be quite sure of a Palestinian locale. The attempts to ascribe the work's origin to some language other than Hebrew generally imply its composition in some non-Jewish territory. There is also the danger of circular reasoning: we must argue from the book's style and contents to arrive at a plausible conclusion as to its setting. But then do we have the right to turn the argument around, and draw on the proposed setting to interpret or clarify the many obscurities of the text? The present writer faces this challenge with his eyes open, fully conscious of the temerity involved, and the danger of multiplying hypotheses or piling one speculation on another. He cannot claim more than probability—but, he hopes, a solid one—for the opinions here expressed.

With some notable exceptions (who would date the book as pre-Exilic) the majority of present-day critics who have discussed the question of the book's origin would locate it in the post-Exilic era of Israelite history; that is, with the sixth-century Exile as a *terminus post quem*. Space does not allow citation of the evidence here: it is a combination of arguments from language (Aramaisms, neologisms preparing for Mishnaic Hebrew), quotations from other books (especially Jeremiah), and from content (the problems of retribution and innocent suffering, which in Israel appear to have come to life after the experience of the Exile). One might even bring the terminus down a little further: not before 500 B.C. It seems that the reconstruction of the temple (520-515 B.C.) marked a surge of optimism as regards the future, evidenced in Haggai and Proto-Zechariah, which was succeeded in the first half of the fifth century (till the time of Nehemiah) by discouragement and demoralisation. 500-445 B.C. would seem a more likely period for such a radical and probing criticism as the Book of Job. But perhaps it is to be dated later. To fix a *terminus ante quem* is even more difficult and uncertain. One solid argument is a negative one: Job shows no trace of Hellenistic influence. The latter is very plain in Sirach (*c.* 200-175 B.C.) and traceable in Ecclesiastes

3

(mid-third century?), i.e., in the way the latter formulates his problems. Job therefore antedates such influence, which not only was prevalent in Palestine after (about) 300 B.C. but probably had made itself felt some decades earlier. One may envisage the composition of Job as occurring, most probably, between 500 and 350 B.C., and this writer would be inclined to put it, within that period, early rather than late.[1]

The question of locale is of less importance, but more easily settled by the evidence of language. A book written in Hebrew in the fifth century could expect only a limited reading public, within a limited area. (This was long before the nationalistic revival of the language that was to be witnessed in the Maccabean era.) It is most probable that the work was composed within the little post-Exilic province of Judea, say within a 25-mile radius of Jerusalem; and very likely that the author was a Jerusalemite, especially if he flourished after Nehemiah's refortifying of the city in 444 B.C. I here pass over without argument various proposals that have been made, to see in Job a translation from some other language, in particular Arabic. None of them seems to be plausible.

2. THE POLITICAL BACKGROUND

From the time of Cyrus's conquest of Babylon, 539 B.C., the Western provinces of the one-time neo-Babylonian empire had been under Persian rule, and from the time of Darius the Great (522-486 B.C.) the little province of Judea had made part of the fifth satrapy, governed from Damascus. Devastated and partially depopulated by the Babylonian punitive expeditions of 597 and 588, the territory had nevertheless gradually revived and been resettled by peasant farmers: some were native Judeans, local survivors of the catastrophe, others were Edomite immigrants, infiltrating from the south. Furthermore, from 538 on, a movement of 'return' to the land of their ancestors began among the Jews resident in Mesopotamia and to some extent among those dispersed elsewhere. We cannot estimate the numbers involved; but this proto-Zionist movement continued sporadically for several generations. It made possible the rebuilding of the Jerusalem temple, on the mount just north of the city, in 520-515 B.C.; it produced the fortification and repopulation of the city itself, under Nehemiah, in 444 B.C.; and at an uncertain date, probably in the late fifth century, it saw the introduction and enforcement, by royal authority, in Jerusalem and its territory, of a revised version of the Mosaic law.

This is good evidence that the Persian authorities were not interested in imposing any alien law code upon a subject people. Provided the taxes, whether in metal or in kind, were duly collected and forwarded to the royal treasury, and the population refrained from political or military agitation, it is evident that the tolerant Persians left the Jews to 'run their own show'. There was a governor in Jerusalem, the *peha*, responsible directly to the satrap of Syria; but the only ones whose names we know, Zerubbabel and Nehemiah, were themselves members of the Jewish community. There was also, of course, the high priest of the temple—Joshua and his successors—whose place and authority must have been officially recognised. And at least once we hear of a species of 'royal commissioner', namely Ezra the Scribe, empowered to promulgate and enforce 'the book of the law of God'. The date of his arrival, however, remains uncertain, and (in spite of Neh. 8:9) it appears probable that he and Nehemiah were not in Jerusalem together.

The political situation, then, of the Jewish population of southern Palestine under Persian rule was favourable and even prosperous. This is confirmed by the absence of unfavourable propaganda, in our sources, against the Persian kings: there is nothing comparable to the denunciations against preceding imperial powers, such as Nahum's tirade against Nineveh or the Psalmist's curse (Ps. 137) on Babylon. Only the Book of

Esther reflects some experience of anti-Semitism within the Empire, but in that rather fantastic story King Ahasuerus is happily converted to be Defender of the Jews. The province of Judea, especially after the rigorous reform activities of Nehemiah and Ezra, presumably had a relatively homogeneous population, in which the Jews would be the predominant element.

3. THE RELIGIOUS BACKGROUND

To appreciate the religious situation of these fifth-century Judeans we must go back a full hundred years. The first decades of the sixth century had been the years of disaster: between two successive deportations (in 597 and 586) of property-owners and officials, there had been an eighteen-month siege of Jerusalem, with all the suffering and starvation that that involved; the countryside had been devastated; finally temple, palace and city had been looted, set on fire, and demolished.

A pitiful band of survivors, half-starved and with only what they could carry on their backs, were mobilised for a trek of 1,000 km through the Syrian desert and along the Euphrates valley. It has often been suggested that such a passage as Job 12:17-25 may have been inspired by the tradition of that Death March. It may indeed be so; however, such forced migrations were no rarity, in the history of the Fertile Crescent. Information on the experience of the Exile is scanty; we get only tantalising glimpses, in Baruch's narrative in the Book of Jeremiah, in some personal reminiscences of Ezekiel, and in the Book of Lamentations, which is an attempt to make sense, theologically, out of this unimaginable disaster. Such was the experience of the first generation of exiles, down to about 550 B.C. Then, after the death (562 B.C.) of the great Nebuchadnezzar, there appeared Cyrus the Persian, to be rapturously greeted by the Second Isaiah as the Lord's chosen instrument and servant for the redemption of his people. The political consequences we have noted above. The religious ones we can only infer, for lack of direct evidence. For instance, it was surely in Babylonia, in the sixth century, that synagogue worship developed, to meet the people's need for community ritual. Whether actual buildings were erected or adapted for the purpose, we cannot say; Ps. 137 obviously pictures an outdoor service on the bank of a river or canal, but that presumably was early in the period. There is nothing to suggest that the exiles ever undertook to build a temple or to offer sacrifice, away from 'the place which the Lord your God has chosen'. Presumably the Deuteronomic food laws were already known, and—along with the observance of Sabbath and the circumcising of male children— would assume great importance as effective means of keeping the community united and separate from the idolaters. We have only slight indications of the literary activity that went on among them, but it must have been intense. A penultimate 'edition' of the Pentateuch (the Priestly Code not being added till Ezra's time), very likely the whole Deuteronomic history (Joshua-Kings), and some at least of the prophetic texts must have been collected and edited in the period of the Exile.

4. THE SAPIENTIAL BACKGROUND

At the time of the composition of Job, Wisdom literature in the ancient Near East had a long and creditable history to look back on; it can be traced, both among the Sumerians and among the Egyptians, back into the third millennium B.C. But all that need concern us here is its relatively recent development in Israel: what Hebrew writings would have been available to, and likely to have influenced, our author? To start with one fairly clear example: he must surely have read Jeremiah, since his great threnody on human life in chapter 3 is clearly an elaborate variation on Jeremiah's 'curse of his day' in Jer. 20:14-18. If he read that, he must have read the rest of the 'Confessions', including the poignant protest in Jer. 12:1ff. Here already he may have found encouragement to put in the mouth of a religious and God-fearing hero the complaints and reproaches that have impressed and even startled readers ever since. Jeremiah, too, was personally blameless; he suffered through the faithlessness of his people, and for their sin. He was an innocent victim of collective guilt, a long-standing and familiar concept among the Semites, but one that he (and Ezekiel) was later to try to correct and abolish among the survivors (Jer. 31:29f.; Ezek. 18:2f.). That is, the doctrine was being used by the 'younger generation' to affirm their own innocence—and implicitly, the injustice of the Lord in thus punishing them. Naturally, our author, intending to treat the problem of the suffering of the just in its most stringent form, had to isolate his hero from any possible solidarity with a sinful people or family. He did that, as we know, by making clear that Job is a non-Israelite and by stressing that there were no unexpiated sins in the family that might have occasioned his afflictions (see Job 1:5).

Other texts that might well have served to focus our author's insight would be the sapiential psalms, in particular Pss. 1, 37, and 73. The first of these, of course, may be of later composition than the book, if it was designed to function as an introduction to the completed Psalter. Even so, it clearly echoes long-standing tradition and doctrine, when it calmly and confidently lays down the principle of retribution in this life, as though no doubts had ever been cast on it and no problem existed as to its validity. 'In all that [the righteous] does he prospers. The wicked are not so. . . .' This is simply stated, as a principle needing no validation. But Ps. 37:25 appeals to experience:

> I have been young, and now am old;
> Yet I have not seen the righteous forsaken
> or his children begging bread.

We are inclined to say that the Psalmist must have lived a rather sheltered life, or else been singularly unobservant; but his dictum is not only naive, it is actually dangerous. Because, if his attention were forcibly drawn to a man forsaken, whose children had to beg, the temptation would be to retort: 'That just shows that he was not righteous in the first place.' And there is the trap into which the friends of Job fall. Beyond the (legitimate) religious principle, 'He who sins shall suffer', they take the fatal extra step of adding, 'And he who suffers must have sinned'. Compare the problem posed by Jesus' disciples, and his correction (John 9:1-3).

To do the sages justice, this exaggeration had already been implicitly but forcefully rejected, for example in the Book of Proverbs: 'He who oppresses a poor man insults his Maker, but he who is kind to the needy honours him' (Prov. 14:31); 'he who is kind to the poor lends to the Lord,/and he will repay him for his deed' (*ibid*. 19:17; see 15:16f., 16:8, 19; 17:1, 5, etc.). Thus poverty, though undeniably an affliction, is not necessarily a sign of God's displeasure, in fact the poor are his special friends. But if that was true of poverty, why might it not be equally true of sickness or persecution or any other suffering, which traditionally was to be interpreted as consequence of sin or penalty or folly?

The psalmists referred to were struggling to reconcile and do justice to two quite different and partially opposed doctrines or visions of the moral universe in which human beings exist. Traditionally the wisdom that they acquired and formulated and transmitted was conceived as a distillation of generations of human experience. It was supposed to rest on a basis of trial and error, of successful and verified experiment, arriving at the principles of order and causality according to which the world operates. That is, it was supposed to be reasoning *a posteriori*. But inevitably, once wisdom discussions rose above the level of the material world, to deal with questions of ethics and morality, theological principles *a priori* began to intrude. The uniqueness of the God of Israel, his omnipotence and sole causality, above all his concern for justice and his condemnation of injustice and immorality—these were beliefs held on the ground of the covenant theology and Israel's collective experience of the Deity. In this theology, great stress was laid on the rewards promised for obedience and the penalties threatened for disloyalty. Since the psalmists and sages we are considering were Israelites even before they were wise men, they naturally strove to unify their beliefs into a synthesis.

The most profound and at the same time the most realistic of the Wisdom psalms is Ps. 73, which anticipates the Joban statement of the problem, and the direction at least in which a solution may be sought. Ps. 73 has the form of a thanksgiving, recited by a man who has successfully emerged from a crisis of faith. In view of the prosperity and power of certain irreligious apostates, contrasted with his own misery and weakness, he came seriously to doubt the ability—or the willingness—of the Lord to keep his covenant promises. Such scepticism threatened to undermine his loyalty to the ancestral religion. What saved him and restored his faith was a double insight—which he received as a gift from God: on the one hand the brevity of the apostates' prosperity, soon to end in disaster; on the other, the permanence of his own relation to the Lord, in itself a greater treasure than any material wealth.

Whether Ps. 73 is the record of a real historical crisis in one man's life, or simply a liturgical composition giving dramatic and individualised expression to a fairly common religious experience, is hard to decide; in view of the cultic character and purpose of the Psalter as a whole, the second alternative seems more likely. In either case, we have here a text which may well have contributed to the composition of the Book of Job.

In summary, the time of this book's appearance was a period of crises and of *aggiornamento* for the Jewish community, a time when one world had passed away and another was struggling to be born. A hallowed and seemingly permanent religious and social structure had collapsed, and the survivors had to learn to adapt themselves and find their way in this new world. A new examination of the old retribution theology was called for, and a revision of its over-simplified concept of retribution: that (among other things) is what the Book of Job aims to provide.

Note

1. This view agrees substantially with the conclusions arrived at by J. Lévêque, in his helpful discussion 'La Datation du livre de Job' *Supplements to Vetus Testamentum* 32 (1981) 206-219. He dates the bulk of the work between Proto-Zechariah and Malachi, with the Elihu-speeches and ch. 28 as having been inserted later.

Philippe Rouillard

The Figure of Job in the Liturgy: Indignation, Resignation or Silence?

AFTER SUFFERING so many misfortunes, after losing all his possessions, all his children and even his health, after putting up with the moralising of his friends, was Job to undergo further disgrace? Was he to be transmitted to posterity under a false identity, disfigured by the Christian tradition and by the liturgy in particular?

For centuries—from the ninth to the twentieth to be precise—most Christians were unable, or forbidden, to read the Bible. The only way in which they knew anything at all about Job was through the liturgy: his cries of indignation or resignation were heard in the readings of the Office for the Dead, on the occasion of a burial or an anniversary. In the clerical world—a milieu both privileged and influential—Job appeared in a different, and less dramatic, context: the readings for Matins during the first two weeks of September. In what way, then, was Job presented by the liturgy? Was the portrait accurate or faulty, authentic or altered for the edification of the Christian people? And how is he presented today?

Our study will not deal with the liturgies of the Eastern rite: these are not well known by the Western world and their treatment of Job is very discreet. We will concentrate on the Roman liturgy, particularly that of the long period from the middle ages to Vatican II, for this traditional liturgy gave birth to the Christian mentality. We will also study the liturgy from Vatican II to the present day, as the recent reform of the Missal and the Breviary has significantly modified the context in which the Book of Job is read. This reform has not yet had time to transform the Christian mentality, but we must be mindful of its intention to alter the liturgical profile of Job. In this article we will examine systematically the portrayal of Job, in the liturgy for the dead and the liturgical year, comparing the situation before and after Vatican II.

1. THE LITURGY FOR THE DEAD: A MAN DIVIDED

Why did you bring me forth from the womb? Why do you not acquit me of my iniquity? Why do you count me as an enemy? From the seventh to the mid-twentieth century, the Office for the Dead resounded with the critics and questions of Job. It is remarkable—and, for the Roman liturgy, exceptional—that in the Matins for the Dead the nine readings were taken from one book of the Bible: Job.[1] Out of all the characters in the Bible, Job was chosen as the best spokesman for men struggling with the enigma, or scandal, of death. Nonetheless, we must try to understand the meaning of the liturgical reading of Job; this meaning is revealed as much in the choice of pericopes as in the choice of responses following each of these passages. The passages chosen for the nine lessons are as follows: Job 7:16-21; 10:1-7; 10:8-12; 13:22-28; 14:1-6; 14:13-16; 17:1-3, 11-15; 19:20-27; 10:18-23. In all of these Job is speaker: the Liturgy for the Dead pays no heed to the speeches of Job's friends, or even to those of God. It is Job, and Job alone, who speaks, and, apart from one passage—19:20-27—only God is addressed with questions of astonishment or vehemence: You fashioned man in such a marvellous way, you gave him life—why then do you treat him so callously, with a sort of hostility? God seems to act no longer as God but as a man, vindictive and heedless of all mercy. How can God be the friend of man, yet accept the scandal and the injustice of a death that seems to issue in nothingness? Why has man been given this poisoned gift, a life so obviously brief, precarious and insignificant? No effort was made to temper the reproaches of Job in the Christian liturgy and even his most sombre lines were not censured:[2] 'If a man die, shall he live again' (14:14), or 'If I say to putrefaction "You are my father" and to the worm "my mother" or "my sister", where then is my hope?' (17:14-15). The horizon appears to be completely hemmed in.

In the penultimate reading, however, an unexpected dawn suddenly breaks and with a vigour which the liturgy hastens to make its own, Job affirms his faith in the resurrection and his certitude of seeing God after death. This astonishing passage is as follows (19:25-27):

> For I know that my Redeemer lives,
> and at last I will rise from the earth;
> I shall put on my skin again,
> and in my flesh I shall see God,
> whom I shall see for myself,
> and my eyes shall behold, and not another.
> This is the hope that is in my bosom.

We must leave it to the exegetes to explain how so lucid an affirmation, with a text which varies significantly from version to version, could pierce through the darkness of the Book of Job.[3] Yet, for a time when no particular importance was given to scientific exegesis, it is not surprising that this declaration was so gladly incorporated into the Christian liturgy: it is a profession of faith and hope, coming from a man who has suffered deeply from inquietude and anguish in face of the mystery of death.

What is surprising, on the other hand, is that in this context the reading from Job does not end on this note of hope. The ninth and final reading of the Matins for the Dead actually returns from chapter 19 to chapter 10, and thus from light to deepest darkness: Job declares that it would be better for him never to have been born, to have gone straight from womb to grave; then he would not have to go to this 'land of gloom and deepest darkness, in the shadow of death, where not order but external horror reigns' (10:18-22). It is with this amazingly horrific vision that the liturgical reading of Job ends. Could it be possible that the reading originally ended with the luminous vision of chapter 19, and that this tragic postscript was added during a time of terror (twelfth to thirteenth century), an era which also produced the Dies Irae? This is a theory well worth examining.

As mentioned above, the responses following each lesson in the liturgy provide the key to a Christian interpretation of the Book of Job. This rule, which applies to all readings of the Divine Office, is particularly relevant to the Matins for the Dead. The

B

first reading is fairly sombre: its response is taken from the most luminous lines of chapter 10, modified to form a more explicit act of faith. In this way

> 'I *know* that my *redeemer* lives'
> becomes 'I *believe* that my *redeemer lives*' and
> 'and in my flesh I will see God' becomes
> 'and in my flesh I will see God, my Saviour'.

In the second lesson God is reproached for his vindictiveness; the response evokes the resurrection of Lazarus. The response to the bitterness of Job is thus one of confidence, reinforced by other passages from the Old Testament, or even from the Gospel. The readings from Job expresses the quite legitimate anguish of the deceased; the responses, spoken or sung by the congregation, form the reply of the Choir, which puts to full use the most confident words of its interlocutor and makes discreet reference to the Gospel. It is true that the other replies remain much more sombre in tone, restricted to pleas for God's mercy on the formidable Day of Judgment.

When all is said, Job was not disfigured or manipulated by the Liturgy for the Dead. He was heard and respected, but as his cries resounded over the centuries the Church attempted to answer them with a more enlightened faith.

What has happened to Job in the liturgy resulting from Vatican II? At first sight he would appear to have disappeared completely. The three biblical readings of the Office for the Dead are now taken from the Epistle to the Corinthians, and these proclaim the most explicit faith possible in the resurrection of Christ and Christians. However, Job does still have some say in the chapter, if only to a very limited extent. By a strange inversion, he now figures in the responses to two of these readings. The first one resumes the well known passage 19:25-27: 'I believe that my Saviour lives', while the other retains a more sombre tone.

The new Liturgy for the Dead thus broke with a thousand-year-old tradition. It was felt that Job had done his time, that his speech was no longer relevant to the Christian celebration of death and that St Paul was the better spokesman. There was, no doubt, a wish for a more Christian, and more reassuring, message. It is conceivable also that in passing from Latin to vernacular the language of Job, rich in imagery and pathos, might disconcert the faithful rather than offer them help. But is it not regrettable that this voice, so great and full of humanity, has now been reduced to silence and that the figure of Job has virtually disappeared from the liturgy which accompanies man on his journey from this world to the next? It is true that the Missal permits Job 19:1.25-27a. to be read at Masses for the Dead: 'For I know that my Redeemer lives . . .'. But this over-catechised Job is no longer the Job of the Bible.

2. THE LITURGICAL YEAR: FROM RESIGNATION TO SILENCE

In the Roman liturgy, Job does not only appear in the context of death. For a few weeks in the autumn he makes a regular and less dramatic appearance in the Breviary or Missal.

For centuries there was no shortage of time for celebrating Divine Office, and all of the Old Testament books were read at Matins over the year. Thus, for two weeks towards the end of summer, Job was read in its entirety. The Roman Breviary of Pius V retained a copious reading of the Book of Job for the first two weeks in September, covering chapters 1 to 9 and extracts from chapters 27 to 42. This anthology preserved the whole structure of the story of Job, from the calamities at the beginning to the restoration at the end. Preference was given to the passages where Job recognises the transcendance of God and the speeches of God were of considerable importance. On the other hand, Job's indignation was barely touched upon, as if it almost did not happen; surprisingly, the text on the resurrection (19:25-27) did not figure in this context, as if it was reserved for the Office for the Dead.

In this autumn mediation, Job appeared with regard to the problem of suffering rather than the enigma of death, complaining about his friends rather than about God. In the liturgy, however, this reading was modified significantly by the responses and the antiphons of the Magnificat, exalting the patience and submission of the holy man Job, and line 1:22 was repeated as a refrain: 'In all this Job did not sin nor say anything stupid against God.' This liturgical presentation removed the Job in revolt, replacing him entirely by Job the patient model of Christian resignation. The preacher found it only too easy to use so edifying an example of submission to God's will, particularly manifest on occasion of misfortune and bereavement: 'The Lord gave and the Lord has taken away; blessed be the name of the Lord.' This line (1:21) supposedly summarises the whole reaction of Job towards misfortune, exempting or dissuading the people from hearing the rest of the speech. The intermediate role of the clergy ensured that the faithful heard only this call to resignation.

Will the post-conciliar liturgy eventually provide us with a more complete and balanced picture of Job? In the present breviary the greater part of the book is read continuously either for two weeks every year or for three weeks every two years.[4] The most notable cuts concern chapters 15-17, 25-27 (the second and third cycles of the speeches) and 33-37 (the speech of Elihu). These two or three weeks allow Job, his friends and, of course God, all the time to have their say. People who celebrate the Divine Office are exposed to a fortnight of Job.

The importance given to Job in the Missal, however, is quite insufficient. As regards Sunday Mass, where the Old Testament is read over three years, he appears on a mere two occasions, in the course of Cycle B. On the fifth Sunday of Ordinary time Job 7:1-7 is read, a meditation on human frailty, dictated by the Gospel about healings; on the twelfth Sunday it is Job 38:1-11, four lines on the creation of the sea, to correspond with the narrative of the calmed storm. Over three years, therefore, Christians attending only Sunday Mass hear only two passages from Job, and one of these about the ocean. This is a most derisory treatment, showing the limitations of a lectionary in which the Old Testament is not read for its own sake, but for its often quite artificial relation to the Gospel of the day. Job certainly has grounds for lamentation—the liturgy has deprived him of the right to speak, a right which even Satan did not take away from him!

It is small consolation that Job appears for one week every two years in the Ferial Lectionary (the 27th week of even years), where passages from chapters, 1, 3, 9, 19, 38 and 42 are read. This well chosen anthology does present the essentials of the Book of Job, but only to a small minority of Christians—those attending Mass on a daily basis.

What conclusions can be drawn from this study? Since at least the ninth century the Church has had ceaseless recourse to the Book of Job for her liturgy. She has obviously offered a specific interpretation of this book—as she has done with all the books of the Bible, the gospels included—by the importance she has given to it and the way in which she has presented it. For more than ten centuries the Church asked Job to be spokesman for all the deceased of the West, expressing simultaneously the anguish of the man and the fervent hope of the believer. In the Liturgy for the Dead, Job is no model of resignation, and the well known line 'The Lord has given and the Lord has taken away; blessed be the name of the Lord' does not figure in this liturgy. Job appears instead as a man divided, torn between a feeling of revolt and a sudden enlightened certainty of the resurrection to come.

The inexact and edifying image of a Job submitting, almost silently, to the divine will appears in another part of the liturgy, but only to curtail and deform the complete message of Job.

In the post-conciliar liturgy, Job's role has been significantly modified: his words have been almost entirely removed from the celebration of death; when he does speak it is to a selective audience (at Divine Office or Daily Mass) as he has been refused virtually all opportunity to address the Sunday congregation.

To conclude, the Roman liturgy does not present one image of Job, but a diversity of images. This diversity of images corresponds to a diversity of human attitudes, or rather to the complexity of the believer's interrogation and reaction in face of the mystery of suffering, which reaches its crisis in the mystery of death.

Translated by Patricia M. Newton

Notes

1. The oldest Roman funeral ritual, going back to the seventh century, does mention an office celebrated in church in the course of which 'psallant psalmos vel responsoria vel lectiones de Iob' (Ordo XLIX, 7; *Les Ordines Romoni* ed. M. Andrieu, IV, p. 530).

2. All biblical quotations here are from the Catholic edition of the *Revised Standard Version* to the extent that they render the Vulgate text used by the liturgy.

3. See, e.g., J. Lévêque *Job et son Dieu* (Paris 1970) pp. 467-489.

4. There are in fact two cycles of biblical readings: in the first, which lasts for a year, Job is read during the eighth and ninth weeks of Ordinary time; in the second, which lasts two years, the fifteenth, sixteenth and seventeenth weeks (also of Ordinary time) are given over to Job.

PART II

The Profile of Revolt

Claus Westermann

The Two Faces of Job

ANYONE READING the Book of Job must be struck by the contrast between Job's attitude to God in the prose-narrative which forms the framework of the Job drama, and his attitude in the drama itself. In the narrative he is the patient, humble, godly man, resigned to the fate which God has appointed for him; in the drama he accuses God, rebels against him and resists the fate which God sends him.

The usual explanation for this opposition is a literary one: the framework is an ancient folk-tale whereas the drama of Job is independent and has its own validity, since it came into being separately from the framework. Distinguishing two authors does nothing, however, to solve the problem: it merely postpones a solution. Supposing that this theory of two originals is correct, who then is responsible for joining the narrative to the drama? If it is the work of an editor, he must have considered this conjunction to be theologically feasible. It is probable that the author of the Job drama himself set it in its narrative framework, as the end of the book, in particular, suggests. In that case the author of the drama both recognised and intended the opposition between drama and narrative.

If we are to see what the author meant by this, it is essential to understand the two contrasting presentations of Job's relationship to God in their respective contexts. These form the subject of the first part of this essay; in the second part we shall consider how these contexts illuminate the two contrasting attitudes.

1. THE DRAMA OF JOB AND THE STORY OF JOB

(a) The drama of Job is a poem of high quality

Its conception is that of a poet. So the various parts of the Book of Job must be understood as elements of a total and unified work. (On what follows, see C. Westermann *Der Aufbau des Buches Hiob* [Stuttgart ^{3}1978], which includes a survey of recent Job research.) Within its framework (chs. 1-2, 42:7-17) the drama of Job is in dialogue form, first of all between Job and his friends, ch. 3-31, then between Job and God, chs. 31-42 (excepting the speeches of Elihu, 32-37). The first part is framed by Job's complaint, chs. 3 and 29-31. The complaint of ch. 3 was to have been followed by consolation; Job's friends arrive to comfort him. But their attempts at consolation turn into a dispute: the friends accuse Job and reproach him for having complained. They adduce arguments to show that his suffering must be the result of his sin. But Job does not enter into their arguments—rather he turns his complaint against them, for he finds no peace in these arguments (in the three rounds of speeches in chs. 4-27); their teaching rebounds from the hard reality of pain. Chapter 28, like the chorus in a Greek play, accompanies the friends' withdrawal and casts doubt upon their proferred wisdom. The inconclusive dispute having been broken off, Job takes up his complaint again (chs. 29-31) but this time it ends in a challenge to God (31) and thus introduces the second part. God answers the challenge in the speeches of chs. 38-42 and Job humbles himself before him (42).

Seen in this way the dialogue section of the Book of Job really is like a drama. Events take place between three parties—Job, his friends, and God. The poet presents an intrinsically unified action (3-42) which he sets within a narrative framework (1-2; 42). The dominant feature in all this is the complaint; it introduces the dialogue section in ch. 3 and concludes it (chs. 29-31); it connects the dispute between Job and his friends with his appeal to God (31), which grows out of his complaint. Job had appealed to his friends' sympathy, but they failed him. Now he appeals to the ultimate authority. In fact the appeal to God begins right at the beginning of Job's complaint in ch. 3. Here we see Job accusing God—a constant factor in all his complaints. At this point the language of the sufferer's complaint is transposed into that of the lawsuit, since God is both the one who caused Job's suffering and also the judge in the unresolved dispute between Job and his friends. God's reply to Job's complaint and appeal is concealed within the speech of chs. 38-42. One thing emerges clearly: Job now knows that God has heard him, that his appeal has been accepted by God, and so his complaint ceases.

(b) The story of the Good Man Job

There is great significance in the way the Job drama has been fitted into the story of the Good Man Job. This would not be the case if (as many exegetes maintain) the Book of Job is dealing with a problem, an issue of 'thought', illustrated by the 'case' of the man Job. If the author had intended to deal with a problem, the framework narrative would have been a distraction—which is why many exegetes deny it to the author of Job. What the narrative framework means, however, is that the author is not speaking of an imaginary person but of Job, a real living human being, with a name and a particular domicile, just as his three friends are real men with names, living in this particular place.

This is not to say that Job and his friends are 'historical' figures in our sense. The mode of presentation of events in the narrative framework is pre-historical, like that of the stories of the Patriarchs: they are all of a type. Events take place in pre-historical time, the period of the Patriarchs, outside Israel. Other places in the Old Testament mention Job, a good man of ancient times (Ez. 14:14, 20).

The poet makes it clear to his readers that the story he has taken over from the tradition once existed on its own, like the stories of the Patriarchs in Gen. 12-36. Thus he is also making it plain that the story once had its own word to say about Job and that he means it to retain this meaning in the context of the Job drama, even if it does not quite fit with it. The two do not need to agree in everything, as the author starkly illustrates in the fact that 'Satan', who plays an important part in chs. 1-2, does not appear at all in chs. 3-42. He was writing for an audience and a readership who understood this lack of correspondence.

Thus we can proceed to our exegesis. What is said in the prologue and epilogue about Job and his relationship with God will be explained on the basis of the particular context.

2. JOB THE HUMBLE, JOB THE REBELLIOUS

(a) Job in the narrative

The narrative belongs to the wider context of the stories of the Patriarchs. We find a similar story to Job in Gen. 22. Here, too, a man is tested by God and his piety proves itself. There are considerable differences, but the common elements are unmistakable. The basic structure of both stories is the same:

1. God wishes to test his servant.
2. This testing takes the form of a great suffering.
3. The question is whether the sufferer will hold fast to God, i.e., God's word.
4. The servant does hold fast to God, and God removes the suffering.

Another factor in common is that the action takes place within the context of the family. As a story with a theological message Gen. 22 belongs to a relatively late stage in the development of the Patriarchal stories, and Job 1-2 is later than Gen. 22. This is shown by (among other things) the strong tendency to portray Job as a man of exemplary piety. We must understand this feature as part of the historical development of the story; in Gen. 22 it is not so pronounced, although here, too, it is already present. The Job story probably had a pre-history in which this element was not so developed. Originally the story was related, not to give a prime example of humility and submission to God, but to tell of a man, tested by God through grievous suffering, who passed the test. Not one of these stories should be interpreted as if it said everything that can be said about this man.

This is why the author of the Book of Job was not faced with an irreconcilable contradiction. Certainly he was aware of the opposition, but he saw it as one often met with in human life. By prefixing the narrative prologue he was making it clear that Job was a good and God-fearing man. Without the prologue the Job drama could give a false or distorted impression of Job. Precisely because he was aware how bold and uncompromising his picture of the rebellious Job in the drama was, he balanced it with the narrative of the Good Man Job. The resultant tension is a deliberate challenge to his audience.

As for Job's relationship with God, the narrative says that he was 'blameless and upright, one who feared God, and turned away from evil' (1:1; see ch. 31). He looked upon his wealth as the blessing of God. He was accustomed to intercede for his sons when they were celebrating (1:4-5). Learning of the catastrophes in which his sons have perished and he has lost his wealth, he is still able, in his grief and despair, to say

> 'Naked I came forth from my mother's womb,
> and naked shall I return;
> the Lord gave, and the Lord has taken away;
> blessed be the name of the Lord' (1:21).

Then he is visited by the heavy blow of sickness, perhaps leprosy, and in desperation his wife says to him, 'Curse God, and die'; but Job replies, 'Shall we receive good at the hand of God, and shall we not receive evil?'. The narrator concludes each passage with the comment: 'In all this Job did not sin' (2:9-10).

God, who is with Job throughout, has subjected him to two grievous trials, and Job has clung fast to him. The conclusion of the narrative adds that God restores everything to him. If we realise that this was once an independent story, the man's attitude in it seems far less extraordinary than we are accustomed to think. The apparent disproportion only arises when it is joined to the dramatic dialogue, making the erstwhile independent story into a kind of first act of the Job drama. The sharp contrast between Job's words in ch. 2 before the brief interlude of his friends' visit (2:11-13) and his complaint which immediately follows, makes the reader wonder: Is this the same Job?

One little detail in the narrative can make this clear. When Job's wife challenges him to 'curse God and die', he rebuffs her by saying, 'You speak as one of the foolish women would speak'. Job implies that it would be folly to renounce God at this point. He is convinced that it is right and appropriate, in the face of the bitter blows that have come his way, to hold on to God. For him, this is not something strange, extraordinary, remarkable: it is normal. The author of Job was able to prefix the narrative to his drama because he was convinced that both attitudes to God are quite possible in one and the same man.

(b) Job in the Job drama

We have already seen that the dialogue section of the Book of Job is governed by the 'complaint'; the sentences and passages in which Job addresses God are in 'complaint' form. In the Old Testament, but elsewhere too, the complaint, the lament, is the language of suffering. Man's reaction to suffering, pain, disappointment, humiliation and injury has created a special linguistic form, which attains a rich and varied expression in the 'complaint psalms'.

First of all, however, we must be aware of a philological difficulty. The complaint as it is found in the Bible does not occur in our European languages. Until the Christian era the complaint had been part of prayer, part of calling upon God. When, in the Christian churches, the complaint disappeared from prayer, it spelt the end of this linguistic genre. The polarity of complaint and praises was replaced by that of petition and thanksgiving. Now, since the *Sitz im Leben* of the 'complaint' had become restricted to the mourning for the dead, the same word could be used for the latter and for the complaint of the sufferer, although originally they were fundamentally distinct procedures with distinct terms. Once divorced from the context of prayer the sufferer's complaint acquired negative connotations, so that people are urged to 'suffer without complaining!'. Now separate from prayer, the complaint sank to the level of mere reprehensible 'moaning'. We need to be aware of this philological boundary at all times if we wish to understand the Old Testament complaint as a way of calling on God. If, as we are inclined, we automatically see the complaint as something negative, we shall never understand what the Old Testament means by it. There is, however, another side to it. In human society the complaint in law is seen as both positive and necessary. Where some wrong has been done it is right to complain. The innocent sufferer has the right to lodge a complaint. In the Old Testament the complaint before the law and the complaint to God are seen as the same thing addressed to different authorities. And even the court's decision is made in the name of God. For modern man the two have scarcely anything to do with one another. This is important in the case of the Book of Job, because in chs. 12-14 the complaint addressed to God is transformed imperceptibly into the language of the law court.

Latterly a change seems to be in the wind: some of the young churches are taking the initiative in restoring the 'complaint' to its rightful place in prayer. And even in the Western world, under the influence of great catastrophes, there is some change in this regard.

In the Old Testament the complaint is a part of existence, involving as it does pain and suffering. It has its own life; it is a linguistic genre, the result of a long tradition, and exhibits a solid structure in three variations: the I-complaint, the complaint against an adversary, and the complaint to God (see 'Struktur und Geschichte der Klage im AT' in C. Westermann *Lob und Klage in den Psalmen*, [5]1977, pp. 125-164). This threefold shape of the complaint arises out of its being the language of suffering; wherever suffering expresses itself, these three aspects are somehow or other there; this is a well-known fact in psychology and psychotherapy, except that here, instead of the complaint to God, there is the search for meaning. To utter his complaint is the sufferer's privilege, shared by no one else (7:11). The deeper a man sinks into the abyss of suffering, of pain, the less inhibited he may be in reliving his feelings in God's presence, since they only express the depth of his suffering.

If we ignore the fact that these complaints embody a man's torment, if we make them into general, timeless, abstract statements about God, we shall have misunderstood them fundamentally. This is what Job's friends do. They are putting forward a timeless, abstract teaching about God. According to this teaching, what Job says about God in his complaints is wicked. They must condemn him. But nothing of what Job says in his complaint to God about his suffering can be torn from its context without radically altering its meaning. The accusing of God is just such an element. It is a clearly recognisable tendency through all Job's speeches from the first complaint to the last. In his initial complaint in ch. 3 it is restrained, only hinted at. Here Job begins by cursing the day he was born: 'Let the day perish wherein I was born, and the night which said, "A man-child is conceived". . . .' This very beginning (3:1-3, 10) is tending in the direction of accusing God, for behind the day of his birth there stands the God who caused him to be born into this world. The question why he was born at all can only be addressed to God (3:20-23): 'Why is light given to him that is in misery, and life to the bitter in soul? . . .' So far Job is not addressing God, but he is already implying that in his suffering he can no longer understand God's dealings with him.

The first round of speeches (chs. 4-14) develops the complaint to (or against) God in two stages. In Job's first two speeches (chs. 6-7 and 9-10) the complaint exactly corresponds to the inherited pattern of complaint to God in the Psalms (parallels for every element can be found in the Psalms), but, corresponding to the form of the poem itself, all is on a larger canvas. At the beginning of ch. 6 Job apologises to his friends for his language which shocks them: 'For the arrows of the Almighty are in me; my spirit drinks their poison; the terrors of God are arrayed against me' (6, 4). This indirect accusation of God is developed in 7:11-21. This section is introduced in v. 11 in such a way as to make it seem the beginning of the complaint; thus the poet indicates that Job's real quarrel is with God: 'Therefore I will . . . speak in the anguish of my spirit, I will complain in the bitterness of my soul.' Then the complaint begins in direct speech (vv. 12-21). Verse 12: 'Am I the sea, or a sea monster, that thou settest a guard over me?', v. 16b: 'Let me alone . . .', v. 20: 'Why hast thou made me thy mark? Why have I become a burden to thee? . . .'

In Job's second speech (chs. 9-10) the accusation against God is predominant. Here God is shown as the Creator of the world (ch. 9) and of mankind (ch. 10). At the start of his speech Job agrees with Bildad who had argued against him that no one is just before God. Yes, says Job, a man can in no way be just before God (vv. 2-3, 14-16), for he is the Creator of the world: '—who has hardened himself against him, and succeeded?—' (v. 4). But in the praise of the world's Creator (vv. 4-13) Job emphasises the destructive acts of the Lord of creation (vv. 5-7, 12-13); v. 12: 'Behold, he snatches away; who can hinder him? . . .' He draws his own conclusion in vv. 14-15: 'How then can I answer him. . . . Though I am innocent, I cannot answer him; . . .' Now follows his accusation of God in vv. 17-24, 30-35; v. 17: 'For he crushes me with a tempest . . .'; v. 19: 'If it is a contest of strength behold him! If it is a matter of justice, who can summon him?' And this is what Job cries out in the bitter helplessness of his suffering (9:21-31): 'I am blameless; I regard not myself . . . he destroys both the blameless and the wicked. . . .'

The theme of ch. 10 is the creation of man. Job asks God why he destroys what he himself has created. 10:3-7: 'Does it seem good to thee to oppress, to despise the work of thy hands . . . that thou dost seek out my iniquity . . . although thou knowest that I am not guilty?' Verses 8-17 develop this contradiction, vv. 18-19 return to the theme of ch. 3 and ask why God permitted him to be born; v. 18: 'Why didst thou bring me forth from the womb?' In ch. 9 and 10 he accuses God, as the all-powerful Creator of the world, of being a tyrant who destroys people without concern for justice. God the Creator of mankind is accused of pointlessly destroying what he has created. Coming from a God-fearing man, these words are grotesque; one can understand the friends condemning Job as a wicked man. But they can also be seen as the words of a desperate, suffering man, bearing in mind that Job does not jump to the conclusion that God cannot be the world's Creator. He holds fast to God as the Creator of the world and of men, even if he can no longer understand him.

In the third speech, chs. 12-14, Job turns away from his friends and addresses God alone. Here Job's complaint takes on the form of a lawsuit in which he summons God to answer charges of injustice towards him. The 'Why' question coincides with the question as to the juridical basis of God's action. This challenge to God reaches its climax in 13:23-27, where the various complaints are brought to a focus.

The citation of God is introduced in ch. 12 by the theme of God as the Lord of history. The psalms of praise (e.g., Ps. 33) speak of God's majesty in these terms: he is the Creator and Lord of his creation, as in Job 9-10; he is the Lord of history, as in Job 12. This correspondence shows clearly that we have here not only the themes but also the structures of the Psalms. The way the theme of God as the Lord of history is developed in 12:13-25 is a magnificent continuation of the Psalm theme, but it emphasises the element of the incomprehensible in God's action in history; v. 13: 'With God are wisdom and might . . .'; v. 14: 'If he tears down, none can rebuild . . .'; v. 16: 'With him are strength and wisdom; the deceived and the deceiver are his . . .'; v. 23: 'He makes nations great, and he destroys them: he enlarges nations, and leads them away.' In 13:1ff. Job turns from his friends and addresses himself solely to God; he introduces his lawsuit (vv. 17-19) and asks God to justify what he has done to him: 13:3: 'But I would speak to the Almighty, and I desire to argue my case with God.' Verse 18: 'Behold, I have prepared my case; I know that I shall be vindicated.' The 'Why?' of the Psalms is sharpened here into a direct question to God about the justice of his treatment of a suffering man. Here a man is demanding justice from God! But this citation of God has suffering for its background; ch. 14 speaks of death as man's destiny. Out of this complaint there arises the desire expressed in 14:13-15 (which shows that, in spite of his accusations, Job holds fast to God): 'Oh that thou wouldest hide me in Sheol, that thou wouldest conceal me until thy wrath be past, that thou wouldest appoint me a set time, and remember me! . . . All the days of my service I would wait, till my release should come. Thou wouldest call, and I would answer thee; thou wouldest long for the work of thy hands.' This concludes the complaint against God at the end of the first round of speeches (chs. 4-14).

In the second round of speeches, chs. 15-21 (Job's speeches are in 16-17 and 19) he reproaches God with being his enemy (16:9-14; 19:7-12). This is all he can do, since God has not responded to his challenge; 16:9: 'He has torn me in his wrath and hated me . . .'; vv. 12-13: 'He set me up as his target, his archers surround me'; 19:7-12: 'Behold, I cry out, "Violence!" but I am not answered; I call aloud, but there is no justice. . . .'

In the third round of speeches (ch. 22-23 and the fragmentary 24-27) there is no longer a clearly-defined complaint against God, but it does form one element in the concluding complaint in ch. 30:20-23: 'I cry to thee, and thou dost not answer me. . . . Thou hast turned cruel to me; with the might of thy hand thou dost persecute me. . . . Yea, I know that thou wilt bring me to death, and to the house appointed for all living.' In ch. 31 Job once more asserts his innocence in an 'oath of purification'. The final complaint which follows amounts to a repetition of the challenge of ch. 13:24-27 but now in the form of a wish, 31:35-37: 'Oh, that I had one to hear me! (Here is my signature! Let the Almighty answer me!) Oh, that I had the indictment written by my adversary! Surely I would carry it on my shoulder; I would bind it on me like a crown; I would give him an account of all my steps; like a prince I would approach him.' When, at the end of the Job drama, as at the end of the first round of speeches, he once again beseeches God to turn to him, putting his plea in the form of a demand for justice, we can see why the dialogue section is always tending towards the petition 'Oh, that I had one to hear me!'. Evidently, we are waiting for something. Will God answer or not? Will God reject or accept the complaint against him?

This is a difficult question. One thing is certain, Job does receive an answer from God in God's speech, chs. 38-41. The assumption made by many exegetes that chs. 38-41 constitute a subsequent addition can be rejected. The construction of the Job drama demands either an answer or its refusal. Possibly, however, the long animal descriptions may have been extended.

The answer begins in 38:1-3 as Job is rebuked. (This is also the purpose of the question put to him in chs. 38-39.) God rejects the accusation that he is Job's adversary, pointing out that Job's place is that of a creature before his Creator. But God's answer has another side to it. It speaks of how the Creator is concerned and cares for his creatures, and thus is an indirect indication that God is actually caring for his creature Job.

Job's last word, however, puts the answer beyond all doubt (42:5): 'I had heard of thee by the hearing of the ear, but now my eye sees thee; . . .' And God's verdict on the friends in the epilogue confirms it: 'You have not spoken of me what is right, as my servant Job has.' This means that God has accepted Job's plea for help—and his accusations.

The author of the Book of Job has also shown this in another, subtle way. He has put into the construction of his work not only the complaint element of the 'complaint psalms' but the other elements as well, including the confession of trust. He uses the latter sparingly: it is found only twice, in 16:19-21 and 19:25-27, but in each case it is part of a speech of Job's in which he accuses God of being his adversary. In these two speeches we find the confession of trust placed right beside the most pointed accusation against God! In 16:18-21 it is juxtaposed to a cry of desperation: 'O earth, cover not my blood'—the cry of an innocent man facing violent death. His blood is to cry out from the ground like that of Abel in Gen. 4. God alone can hear this cry: 16:20f.: '. . . my eye pours out tears to God, that he would maintain the right of a man with God, and that of a man with his neighbour.' But this plea rests on a certainty, v. 19: 'Even now, behold, my witness is in heaven, and he that vouches for me is on high.' There must be someone who will take his part against God's apparently final verdict—and this can be none other than God himself! Thus, against God, he hopes in God.

In 19:25-27 we find the confession of trust in the same context. Job's wish in 19:23f. is the same as that in 16:18, and his certainty is identical with that in 16:19. Thus 19:25: 'For I know that my Vindicator [RSV margin] lives, and at last he will stand upon the earth . . .'; v. 27: 'whom I shall see on my side, and my eyes shall behold, and not another'. If Job still trusts in God in the face of his death, this must mean that, despite his death, he expects God to intervene on his behalf. How?—we are not told. Job is convinced that the impossible can happen. There is something in this trust in God 'in spite of God' which enables the Job drama to point beyond itself.

The final verdict, that Job has spoken correctly of God, means that Job still clung to the God whom he experienced as his adversary. In turn this implies that God even accepts the despairing words of a sufferer who doubts his justice, if only he will cling to him in this abyss of despair.

This is the solution to the two faces of Job. The pious, humble man, submissive to

God's will, and the desperate man who resists God—these are one and the same person, in touch with both possibilities. But we must note that in the dialogue section it is not suffering as such which causes Job to rebel, but what the friends say. They see the suffering and the words to which it gives voice as evidence that Job is a godless man. He accepts neither this, nor the view that the degree of suffering must correspond to the degree of the transgression for which God is punishing him. And when God leaves Job to his suffering and hence to his deathward path, he seems to be on the side of the friends. But then he answers. And in his answer he comes in on Job's side and takes up his cause. God turns in love to the Job who had so gravely accused him.

We need to attend to this complaint, however, on another plane, the plane on which the poet is speaking to his contemporaries. It was a time of collapse. Israel was a state no longer. The Kingdom and the Temple were no more. This had put an end to the automatic assumption hitherto that God was in control of everything. It was much easier to believe that God was responsible for all events in a small, manageable sphere of life, protected on all sides. Once these protective walls had fallen, how could all that took place in the wide-open and unprotected arena of life—all that was rich and productive, as well as all that was terrible beyond belief—be related to God, be conceived as his activity?

This was the new situation which the author of 'Job' portrays in his elaboration of the theme 'God as the Lord of history' in 12:13-25: 'If he tears down, none can rebuild; if he shuts a man in, none can open.' This collapse can be compared, to some extent, to the collapse which has affected the Christian churches of the West as a result of industrialisation and especially through the fact that, thanks to the media, every Christian can participate in all the catastrophes and atrocities of the world. In their changed situation, a certain group of people in Israel felt that the godfearing could only survive if they held on to a rigorous and infallible doctrine of retribution, the view that God blesses the good and punishes the evil. Job's friends put forward such a view. Consequently Job must be a sinner and they must condemn him. But the conclusion of the Book of Job says that the friends have not spoken well of God. The poet of 'Job' is convinced that this teaching is no longer relevant to the new reality, and puts forward a view of God which takes account of the world as it really is. In ch. 21, the only speech in which Job takes up his friends' arguments, he points to the experience which is available to everyone (21:29): the 'wisdom' tirelessly proclaimed by his friends, that the good live well whereas wicked men must have a hard time, is false. So Job reproaches them: 'How then will you comfort me with empty nothings? There is nothing left of your answers but falsehood' (21:34).

In the figure of Job the poet shows the grave dilemma which may have to be faced if we are to affirm our belief in the God of the real world in the face of unintelligible and inexplicable suffering. We must take Job's dilemma seriously, and if we are not likewise at a loss when confronted with the incomprehensible suffering of the world, then our theology is dubious.

Translated by Graham Harrison

François Chirpaz

Ernst Bloch and Job's Rebellion

'IT IS above all in the Book of Job that the remarkable reversal of values begins, the discovery of utopian power at the heart of the religious sphere: a man can be better, can behave better than his God. Job has not merely given up worship but he also leaves the community: it is an all-out attack.'

'The simplest solution is to recognise that there always exists in the world a new exodus which compels us to leave the established order, a hope which is linked to anger and which finds itself to be based on the actual possibilities of a new being. Through these we have a hold on the future, on a process full of promises—but also very uncertain, though unceasingly brimming with solutions: its solution, our solution.'[1]

The figure of Job occupies a decisive place at the centre of Ernst Bloch's *Atheism in Christianity*. He is the central figure in the contestation with Yahweh, the Promethean moment when man rises up alone in face of God's omnipotence. But he does not yet embody what will only be made manifest with Jesus the heretic, the Son of Man by whom what had been abandoned to the hypostasis of an omnipotent God is reincorporated in the human. It is in fact with Jesus that for Bloch the new and definitive exodus is realised whereby man at last leaves God to come to be with himself. Job is himself not yet the Messiah, he is only waiting for him who will come to avenge the suffering Yahweh imposes on him: he is the one through whom there is brought about the departure from worship and the departure from the community of those who enjoy the position of servitude under the theocratic law.

He is the central figure, proportionate to the violence of the words of the rebel bent under the weight of the suffering imposed on him, without understanding what game it is that God is playing with him. He is not yet the man who organises his own rebellion, as will be done later by the Messianic movements. Nevertheless he is for Bloch the first to have the audacity to take as far as he does the exodus from the God whom his friends recognise and whom the priesthood is bent on imposing.

Job is the rebel who dares to defy God himself in all his power. He is the brother of Prometheus who is another to have the audacity to defy the power of Zeus and who dares give the sacreligious message to a terrified Hermes: 'I hate all the gods—they are under an obligation to me, and through them I am being treated iniquitously.' He is the figure of the rebellion which is only made by someone with the audacity of man's freedom when this is manifested in its truth. Man is man in the act by which he breaks all domination imposed from outside, when he reappropriates for himself his being and at

23

last understands that his destiny cannot be controlled by a superior power outside the world and outside history but that he is man in history. The dimension of man is the time of history, and the time of history is the not yet determined beforehand.

The major axis underlying the totality of Bloch's work, from his first studies of *Thomas Müntzer* and *The Spirit of Utopia* to his masterpiece *The Principle of Hope* and *Atheism in Christianity*, develops and amplifies the theme that to consider human reality in the truth of its being is to understand it as the constant movement of a transcendance which, during the first stages of human history, man dare not recognise as belonging to him as his own. Hence he willingly believes those who divert his gaze from the earth where men fashion their history in order to place this action in a transcendance, a reality outside the world, outside time, outside man, and surpassing them.

To reappropriate for oneself the act of transcendance, in other words the sovereign power of freedom, without having recourse to a transcendance exterior to oneself: this is the positive movement of human history. It is then that man understands what he is in his being and the effective reality of history, a process of growth that has not yet revealed how his possibilities all fit together. This growth is a movement that is going on but has not yet wholly realised its possibilities, to the extent that man has not succeeded in establishing the law of freedom alone, to the extent that he is forced to submit to a law imposed by others who are his masters and to live under a God who is the representative of this very heteronomy.

It is by rebellion that man becomes man, rebellion against every reality that is external to the world of man, without having recourse to such a reality: in a word, recognising that the area where his being unfolds is growth that is being realised and is not yet fully realised. Understood in this way, growth can only find the principle of its complete explicitation in Marxism: not in any form of Marxism, but only in that which knows how to keep within a historical perspective of the failure to complete growth. Marxism provides the key to the understanding of this growth, but the indication of this has already been given in the underground stream already present at the heart of the book to which Bloch gives a special place in the history of civilisation, the Bible.

1. THE PRINCIPLE OF INTERPRETATION

The interpretation that Bloch gives of the text of the Bible in *Atheism in Christianity* cannot be separated from a triple thesis which controls the way his work is organised. His thought is resolutely atheist, but it does not identify itself with the traditional atheist theory. It is Marxist, but has no intention of being confused with that current in the kind of socialism that is still half Tsarist. It rests on a reading of the text of the Bible and of the history of Messianic movements, but this reading declares itself from the start as heretical.

The traditional explanation of the fact of religion hardly varies, and the old explanations by Epicurus and Lucretius are still to be found in the age of enlightenment. As far as this is concerned, if man believes in gods, if he needs to turn towards the divine to account for himself and for the world, all this cannot arise from anything other than his fear before the phenomena of the world. What is inexplicable makes one afraid, and fear gives rise to gods to make men feel secure.

Here, Bloch breaks with this tradition. In his eyes it is not their fear but their hope that men invest in religion. In its essence religion is not a hiding place for a mind stricken with fear: it is the first manifestation of the hope that opens man to the real dimension of his being. And it is important to ascribe a place of its own among religious texts to the Bible, 'the most revolutionary of all religious books'.

The inspiration that governs the Old Testament as it does the New is incomprehensible outside the category of hope as much as of that of rebellion. It is of freedom that the Bible speaks, a freedom which leads men not only out of the land of Egypt but of all mythical representations that bind men to a history that is fossilised because it is completely determined before their time. Freedom is exodus, and it reveals to man the as yet undetermined horizon of time, the *eschaton*, as his proper home.

Nevertheless, understanding the biblical text in the perspective of the freedom granted to the *eschaton* of the future open before men demands the implementation of a subversive reading. Aware of the distinctions to be found in the different layers of the text, Bloch adopts them by translating them on the basis of his ideas. The docile interpretation of this history that assigns men to resignation and servitude is opposed by an obstinate interpretation that baulks at this and expresses the murmuring of the rebel. The true depth of the text is revealed by the rebellious attempt at exodus and reparation.

It is deliberately heretical reading (and it is in this way that the interpretations of Job and of Jesus, of the prophets and of John the Baptist, are conducted) because it is carried out 'within the perspective of the Communist Manifesto'. Only this reading, in fact, is able to bring out the genuinely positive aspect of the biblical text, that which demonstrates men's murmurings, their dissatisfaction and their rebellion against the tyrannical theocratic power of God the Father. The underground portion of the text speaks against the authority of the priesthood and of the institutional Church, against that which is on high but weighs on men. This underground portion forms the revolutionary part that speaks to men not of resignation but of opening them up to their future by revealing to them the eschatological horizon.

Only this, however, can bring out an idea which has its origins in Marx's historical materialism. This latter frees men from the necessity of bowing their heads before the transcendance of a supreme reality, and by doing so can see itself assigned 'a role of liberator of mankind'.

Hence the truth of religion is the hope that men invest in it and not their fear. The truth of Marxism is this inspiration which maintains the possible as a fundamental category of reality. The truth of the biblical text is in short this current which never ceases to flow through it and in which man is led little by little to distance himself from the place of the despot of theocracy in order to grant a privileged position to the Messianic aspect: the figure of the Son of Man who leads men out of the power of the heavenly despot in order to return them to themselves. The Son of Man is understood as man having from now on become man, entering upon his humanity by understanding that the future is what he creates, that it depends on him and not on anyone or anything else. It is not then a question of a process of demythologisation, as understood by Bultmann, but of detheocratisation.

2. JOB, OR THE EXODUS OF THE REBEL

Prometheus dared to move outside the law proclaimed by Zeus and did so by taking man's side. Referring to this figure from Greek mythology, Bloch calls Job the Hebrew Prometheus because he dared to stand up against Yahweh by taking the side of the just man condemned without reason to suffer in his life the worst of deaths: a death that is not a death because it does not bring suffering to an end, a life which cannot be a life because Job is compelled to remain only on the fringes of the world of life. He is in the world, but it is as if he were not, because for everyone he has become a subject of horror; he is in life but as if he were not any more because his body has become an unnamable corruption. There is a remarkable likeness between the fates of these two figures.

In Aeschylus's tragedy, in fact, Prometheus has a different stature from that to be found in Hesiod. For the latter he is only a common-or-garden thief guilty of having stolen from the immortals the fire they had been keeping for their exclusive use. For Aeschylus, he is of course the stealer of fire, but far more he is the one who has incurred the hatred of the gods 'for having loved men too much', for having delivered them from the obsession of death, for having sown hope within them and for having given them the means of turning their world into a world where man can live (vv. 234-254 and 439ff.). Prometheus, however, is not a man: he is a god who has defied the power of Zeus (it is as *theos* that he introduces himself to the chorus, vv. 92 and 119).[2] He is thus a god who is opposed to the power of the other gods. Job for his part is a man and it is as a man that he takes his stand before the face of Yahweh.

But who is this lord who is challenged so provocatively by this series of eleven poems, this person who spies on man, this predator who gives the victim he is hunting no respite, this person to whom man never ceases crying but who does not deign to answer? Who is this person who violates man's right and wraps him in his murderous net, who cannot be found anywhere despite an untiring search, who in short makes the just suffer without deigning to take into account his former loyalty? 'The God of the book of Job only appears in heaven with the characteristics of Pharaoh.'

For Bloch, the person who keeps silent throughout the cry of suffering at the end of its tether, who can only answer the long question about the meaning of this trial that man must undergo by physical questions about the world, its origin and its diversity, 'bringing to bear on his subject's limited understanding the cosmic immensity of his impenetrable wisdom', the creator and lord of the world is forced, before the accusation of this suffering man, to reveal himself for what he is: the being above man who cannot have any greater care for man than can the God of Spinoza. Bloch qualifies this by adding *mutatis mutandis*, but for him the analogy is striking: the person who speaks at the end of the poem reveals the person who keeps silent throughout the just man's complaint, and he, like Spinoza's God, 'directs nature according to universal laws and not according to men's particular intentions'.

But is not this God, like that of Spinoza, endowed with reason?—though again like that of Spinoza, the consideration of teleology is foreign to him. The master of the world can only create the suffering of the individual, and if the suffering of the individual raises an appeal against him it is because it is incapable of taking into account the totality of the universe. Such a God is the master of heaven, the one who overhangs in an absolute manner the totality of that which exists and thus, too, man's individual singularity, the giant who towers above man, the same who had wanted to subject Abraham to the despotism of his whim, the God who is jealous of every Promethean impulse, the omnipotent autocrat or the celestial cannibal that will later be found behind the theology of St Paul.

In fact, the God with whom Job's suffering collides, the God whom Bloch tries to bring out by means of his subversive reading which reads the text on the basis of the murmuring of the peoples subject to the divine law, is hardly different from the God whom Hegel, in the theological writings of his youth, thought he could discern in the Jewish awareness of the divine. The God of the Old Testament is not the one who turns towards the world of men but the one who imposes his domination. He is the master, and man can only be his slave. The entire interpretation that Bloch makes use of can be read out of these pages of Hegel: man only sees himself before his God as the slave before his master, and the only relation between the two can be that of domination. 'The whole world, his complete opposite, was kept in existence by a God who remained alien to it, a God in whom no element in nature had a share, but who dominated everything.'[3]

Facing God, this simple theocratic power, the hypostasis of domination, the attitude of the man who does not want to abide by the soothing speeches of his friends (in whom there speaks the voice of the priests) can only be that of a rebel. Heretic and rebel: such is Job, the one who struggles against Yahweh, the one who dares face up to him and demand an account, but still more the one who dares lead the exodus to a place that hitherto has not been reached. He does not merely leave the worshipping community: he leaves Yahweh. He removes man from the necessity of referring to the divine in order to understand himself as man. Job clashes head-on with Yahweh's theocratic power, just as Prometheus clashes head-on with that of Zeus. The accusation he brings against the power of the tyrant rules out of court the lord's claim to exercise this kind of power over man, even if Job himself does not reach the point which will be reached by the rebel Jesus.

In fact, the interpretation of Job that is at the heart of *Atheism in Christianity* cannot be understood apart from the reference to the other forms of rebellion and exodus which slowly force their way through the history the Bible recounts. Something entered history with the serpent—the first steps of the manifestation of the freedom of reason. With the prophets, man learns the power of his freedom capable of stretching as far as his destiny, by discovering the power of his decision. Justice ceases to be something simply conceded from above. But it is with Jesus that the time of man's exodus from the divine reaches its culminating point. The *logos* which has slowly detached itself from its representations in mythology and from the static understanding of the world conveyed by the myths sees itself henceforth identified with man himself. Jesus is the *logos* freed from the matrix of mythology, and at the same time he proclaims himself as the Son of Man. Man no longer needs anything apart from himself alone to establish himself in his being and to understand himself. The Son of Man comes to take over from Yahweh. 'The mysterious title of Son of Man, with all its implications, reinvests in a *humanum* that is still strongly hermetic all the considerable wealth that had been abandoned to the hypostasis of a heavenly Father.'

With Jesus the revolutionary who drove the dealers out of the Temple, man succeeds in reclaiming his being by opening himself to his real dimension, the process of growth that is open before him as the field offered to his potentiality without limit. Jesus discloses the *eschaton* by opening man up to the future that is open and offered to him, thus completing the exodus that was begun well before his time (by Job among others) but never brought to this point.

The long history of rebellion against Yahweh is the history of the egress of thought from the fossilised representation of man's time, from mythology towards the progressive coming of the *logos*, man's egress from the fatality of the system of domination represented in its absolute form by the presence of a being above the world imposing his law from above. The exodus does not thus represent a simple moment in the history of Israel: it is this history itself, the history of human awareness and thought taking up in its hands its own being as its dimension of growth. Man is, in fact, the only reality at the core of history, and history is the sole dimension of man's existence and of his realisation. A history that is not completed and is always kept open: Utopia is what in the present maintains the openness of growth and development. As far as Job is concerned, if he does not yet know that man is only the Son of Man, he knows in any case that man cannot recognise himself as the son of God because this God is not concerned at all about his suffering.

3. JOB'S EFFRONTERY

There can be no question of passing over in silence the incontestable originality of Bloch's thought (considered as a whole and not just in the single work we are dealing with here): giving Marxism an interpretation which preserves the genuinely positive element of the achievements of civilisation, applying a different criterion to the fact of religion (thus differing from Engels, who could only see in it the relic of a pre-history, a simple example of stupidity), for having finally grasped the scale of this remarkable ferment of liberation of existence and thought which the Bible brought into civilisation and history. But on the other hand it is no longer possible to ignore the fact that the grid which Bloch's reading imposes on the texts fails to take into account what they intend to say and what they in fact say explicitly. His interpretation rests on a series of postulates, not to say prejudices. Thus the interpretation given to the figure of Prometheus ignores what is most original about Aeschylus's thought and owes more to the modern reading of the myth than to that of the Greek tragedian. Thus his use of the Hegelian pattern with regard to the Old Testament leads him to adopt without examination the worst commonplaces with regard to the 'God of the Old Testament'. Finally, his vision of history is quite clearly over-inflated: it simply fails to recognise the tragic element in the human condition and the tragic element in history. But above all, to confine ourselves to the subject in hand, his interpretation obliterates the cutting edge of Job's remarks.

Certainly exegesis can tend to soften the cutting edge of these remarks by suppressing their raw and scandalous nature. But Bloch, who only sees in them man's egress from the sphere of Yahweh the despot, goes in for a balanced mutilation.

Job's words have a cutting edge because they are the words of a just man who is suffering and who so boldly challenges his Lord. But the fact is that Job passes through the trial of what in a telling phrase Aeschylus called the 'violent grace' (kháris bíaios, Agamemmon v. 182) which the gods inflict on men: the inevitable violence of the presence of God, because God is not man and, even if the two are close to each other, God remains even in this closeness other than man and therefore always distant. Job's words are violent with regard to his Lord (and thus scandalise his friends), but this is because they spring from an existence that has been completely unhinged, the victim of a trial that separates him from everything and everyone, leaving him in isolation and with no resources in this isolation. To whom could man appeal in the depths of such a trial and who could understand him?

In these words there is an element of overstepping the mark, of effrontery, because they do not just translate suffering but arise from the feeling of the dignity of the man who, in his very suffering, refuses not to understand. It is not a simple manifestation of suffering because it does not stop asking: Why should this be? Who, then, are you, the Lord?

By simply concentrating on the aspect of violence it is easy to turn Job into a rebel. Yet all the same he utters words which one does not find in the mouth of Prometheus. Job may speak to his friends, asking them questions and replying to them, but in fact it is always God himself to whom he is talking. His friends for their part talk about God, but Job never stops talking to God, demonstrating in the depths of his suffering a trust which also has this element of excess.

In fact, Job's effrontery is two-edged: it is to be found in the violence of the accusations he hurls at God, but it is also to be found in the trust which despite everything remains placed in the Lord. Even when most exasperated Job never talks other than to God alone, well aware that, if he who is only a man does not know who God is, he knows equally strongly that despite everything, despite this silence that has gone on so long, God is never completely absent. Trust continues to be placed in him despite everything which occurs to contradict it, and this is nothing other than hope itself.

This kind of effrontery, in contrast to what the Greek tragedians denote by hubris, is not the expression of the pride of someone who has the audacity to harbour thoughts above his mortal condition (as Aeschylus says), but the expression of the love which, in human existence, radically transforms man's relation to his fellow. There is an effrontery which comes from the pride of the man who takes himself as God: there is another which springs from an existence capable of the profoundest attention to the other man and is concerned for him. This kind of effrontery is that of love concerned for the other and turning to the other to break the infernal circle of isolation, something which Dostoïevski was able to describe: the loving presence which has the audacity to turn to another with an attitude of insatiable pity, as Sonia does to Raskolnikov or Alyosha to Kolya.

This kind of effrontery is already present in the biblical text itself—at the very heart of the violent words with which Yahweh appeals to Israel every time Israel is lacking in loyalty to its Lord. It can be heard in the word of the Lord brought to his people through the mouth of the prophets: in the very violence that displays the Lord's wrath there is the effrontery of a love that is recalled and is always there in fidelity. It is the faithful presence of a love which is an anxious and constant concern for man, through everything and despite everything. If man can remain steadfast in hope in the word of the Lord, it is because everything conspires to remind him that despite everything the Lord, too, still hopes in man, transcending every purely human scale.

The cutting edge of what Job says—so different from the texts of Sumer[4]—is so unprecedented that it is always hard to grasp. Yet the first aspect of his effrontery is inseparable from the other. It can only be heard in the constant articulation of this challenge and accusation as well as in that of trust and hope beyond all hope. In one sense, Job offers violence to God (and to a greater extent than Prometheus does to Zeus in the Greek myth), but the Lord recognises the justice of this attitude, because this violence is in the image of that offered by Yahweh to Israel: violence that cannot be separated from tenderness, from trust, and, in a word, from home.

One therefore needs to place oneself where these two forms of effrontery are linked in order to understand the extent to which the violence of the accusation goes beyond simple rebellion. The man who makes the accusation, refusing to give up the hope he has placed in his Lord, is a man in the process of delineating a new awareness of human existence and of this existence in the face of God. What this text brings out is a completely new awareness of the existence of man as man (without anything in common with what we are able to know of surrounding civilisations) and an awareness of man's relation with God that is, strictly speaking, unheard of. Man dares comfort himself before his Lord like a free being, and only a free being can demonstrate such audacity, daring to ask such forceful questions because he is capable of a hope the strength of which is no less: in all this Job is far beyond simple rebellion.

Translated by Robert Nowell

Notes

1. The citations in the text are from the French translation by Eliane Kaufholz and Gérard Raulet (Paris 1978) of *Atheismus im Christentum. Zur Religion des Oxodus und des Reichs* (Frankfurt am Main 1968).

2. For the theology of Aeschylus see Karl Reinhardt *Aischylos* (Bern 1949).

3. *L'Esprit du christianisme et son destin* (Paris 1967) p. 7, French translation of Hegel's *Theologische Jugendschriften* (Tübingen 1907).

4. See two texts, *La Théodicée babylonienne* and *Le Juste souffrant*, in R. Labat and others *Les Religions du Proche-Orient: Textes babyloniens, ougaritiques, hittites* (Paris 1970) pp. 320-341.

Dirk Kinet

The Ambiguity of the Concepts of God and Satan in the Book of Job

INTRODUCTION

THE QUESTION about the picture of God and the concepts of Satan in the Book of Job cannot be answered by way of a simple, undifferentiated approach. The impossibility of giving a clear and unequivocal reply to the question may be put down superficially to the complex history of the book's composition. The work's final editor, at least, was well aware of its pluralistic theology. He deliberately let this plurality in the ideas about God stand, without welding them into a unified dogmatic concept. For the question we are considering here, it is not so important to date the various strands in the book's composition, or to put them in chronological order,[1] so as to trace a line of historical theological development. It is more essential to work out the specific theological questions and conceptions in the individual sections—the frame story, the dialogue, the poem on wisdom, the Elihu speeches and the speeches of God.

1. GOD AND SATAN IN THE FRAME STORY (1:1-2, 10 AND 42:7-17)

The frame story shows the God who is familiar enough to us from Israel's religion and from the documents that have come down to us from her neighbours. Job can atone through precautionary burnt offerings for sins committed against God, perhaps by third persons (Job's children) at feasts (1:5). The offended God allows himself to be pacified again through sacrifice. In the book's epilogue, God vents his wrath on Job's friends. Unlike his servant Job, they have not spoken rightly about him, and he intends to punish them for their false theological notions. He imposes burnt offerings on them as expiation for their guilt, though Job himself can intercede for his friends. God's vengeance and wrath are great, and it is only out of consideration for his servant Job that Job's friends will have nothing worse inflicted on them.

The question about evil and its origin is not under discussion in the frame story. What is in question is the righteousness of Job, about whose merits God and Satan differ. But the context makes it indirectly clear that God bears the ultimate responsibility for evil and injustice in the world; and both Job and his wife are well aware of this (see 1:21; 2:9). A single theological principle runs right through the frame story:

30

the unbroken conviction that retribution is part of the moral order which God will not ultimately rescind. If the innocent Job has to suffer, this can only be a temporary fate which God himself will revoke in the end. Job ultimately receives good as well as evil from God's hand. The divine blessing is shown in Job's new possessions and his rich, fulfilled life. The author of the frame story knows that here he is in conformity with the beliefs of all Israel's neighbours in the ancient Oriental world.[2]

Yet in spite of this, in the frame story the figure of Satan seems to have an exculpatory function. It is not God's own idea to inflict vicissitudes on Job in order to test his religious devotion. Satan is the real instigator, and it is only at his request that God gives him power over Job, so that he can lay hands on Job's possessions, and attack his health and his very life. Satan therefore acts more or less as an independent agent, thereby exonerating God from sole responsibility. We know that the frame story is a revision of earlier material, tailored to a particular function; and it is doubtful whether in the earlier Job legend Satan already played a role.[3] It is more likely that the figure of Satan was only incorporated—and could only be incorporated—at a period when people found it more difficult to push the responsibility for suffering and injustice, and their authorship, on to God alone. In the scene in heaven, Satan is introduced as one of 'the sons of God' (1:6 and 2:1) who gather together 'to present themselves before Yahweh'. The roots of this idea about a divine 'royal household' may well be very old;[4] but here Satan's independent competence and function clearly indicate a post-Exilic origin.[5] In the frame story as we have it, Satan is assigned the role of prosecutor; and in this function he casts doubt on Job's righteousness. But ultimately this serves only to bring out Job's uprightness, for his sense of responsibility and his liberty—especially in adverse circumstances—are all the more emphatically emphasised. No power, not even a heavenly one, can compel the righteous man Job to renounce his faith and trust in God. Before God, Satan called Job's inner liberty in question; but this liberty emerges all the more convincingly in his trials.

2. THE PICTURE OF GOD IN THE POEM

The poem itself is dominated by the dispute between Job and his three friends, Eliphaz, Bilbad and Zophar. A poem on wisdom (28:1-28) and the speeches of Elihu (32:1-37:24) are interspersed in the work. These have to be looked at separately, and so have the speeches of God (38:1-41:25), which, in their own way, are intended to offer a solution to the questions raised by Job.

(a) The Dialogue or Dispute

After Job has cursed the day of his birth (3:1-26) there follows a confrontation with his friends in the form of three cycles of speeches and counter-speeches.[6] Every declaration made by one of his friends is countered by a speech of Job's; and in a final utterance (29:1-31:40) Job again contrasts his present suffering with the happy past. The Job poem is a calculated attack by the author on the traditional dogma of retribution (the correlation between act and destiny). According to this theological idea, the righteous fare well in life and evil-doers come off badly, because every deed involves its natural consequences. This belief was a substantial part of classic theology and popular piety—a basic tenet of Israel's faith and the philosophical outlook of her neighbours. Here, paradigmatically, a suffering person insists on his innocence; and by doing so he shakes the very foundations of the divine order of retribution and justice: 'You are undermining the foundations of faith, making the devout life wholly impossible' (15:4).

The classic doctrinal arguments are summed up in the speeches of the three friends. They depict a God who gives devout men and women hope in suffering (4:6). The person whom God smites he will also heal; so for that reason alone the sufferer can consider himself blessed (5:17-27).

The argument that the fate of the evil-doer leads ultimately to disaster is unusually extensive in its development (8:8-22; 15:7-35; 18:5-21; 20:4-29). God allows no one on earth to suffer unless he is personally guilty (4:7). Moreover no human being is guiltless: 'Not even his angels can he trust, and even the heavens are not clean in his sight' (15:15; see also 4:12-21; 25:1-6). There is no authority that can or will respond to the sufferer's complaint—not even God himself: God is no interlocutor for the person who suffers (5:1-7). So the only possible solution that emerges is unconditional, mute submission before God (5:8-27). No one can presume to know the secrets of the divine will (11:1-12). Anyone who questions God, disputes with him, or rebels against him and the fate he imposes shows himself to be a sinner through his very revolt. Theological and existential questioning of the meaning of events is wicked in itself (15:4ff.). Eliphas's final word to Job is an exhortation to repentence and humility: 'If you return to the Almighty you will be raised up; he abases the man who talks arrogantly, but he helps the one who lowers his eyes' (22:23, 29). Wisdom's classic doctrine cannot be shaken by Job's attacks. Contrary to life and human experience, theology still insists on the dogma of retribution: 'Do you earnestly consider that God perverts justice? Do you believe he does not adhere to his law?' (8:3). It is life and experience which must be wrong; the doctrine itself is never at fault. So Job's friends can only give him one piece of advice: 'You should try to seek God, and pray the Almighty for grace. For if you are truly pure and guiltless, he will surely come to your help' (8:5f.). Anyone who, like Job, incurs guilt before God and man through his persistent questionings can turn to God again and he will restore him (11:13-20).

Job's answer is an indictment of the God of classic theology; he challenges God to face him (finally in 31:35-40). In his answers and rejoinders Job shows that, in the light of his own sorrowful experience and his own self-understanding, he is no longer able to make anything of the picture of the just God. He clings unswervingly the whole time to the rightness of his cause (27:1-6) and sets his interpretation of what he himself is over against the theological theories of his friends—and probably over against his own idea of God as well. So Job's complaint is ultimately directed, not merely against his friends, but against God himself. And his starting-point is his own specific experience: things are going badly for him, righteous though he is; while everything is going well for the wicked (21:7-21). Consequently Job's dominating emotion is total and profound forsakenness. Under these circumstances he does not want to have to go on living. It would even have been better if he had never been born (3:1-26; 6:1-7; 10:18-22). He is disappointed in God, and his disappointment is nourished by the remembrance of happier times, in which he had experienced another, friendly God (29:1-25). Crushed by the suffering imposed on him, he feels bowed down by a merciless, all-powerful God. Against this God he has no defence; with this God he cannot argue: 'O that I knew where I might find him and how I might come to that place! I would lay my case before him, give him my reasons and my proofs. Would he let me feel the greatness of his power? . . . I would pursue my cause with him as one without reproach. That my judge would also have to accept' (23:3-7; see also 9:1-13).

So God's activity as creator and preserver of the world (9:1-13; 26:5-14) is not in itself a reason for human beings to feel in safe keeping. It is rather a reason for profound despair and resignation (12:7-25). God does not hear the cry of those he has created: 'I (Job) am in the right and am not allowed to claim my rights! Should I perhaps appeal for mercy to the One who has already decided on his judgment? Even if he submitted to a legal action—that he would listen to me I do not believe' (9:15f., 21f.). This declaration induces Job to go on to revile God and to accuse him of cruelty: 'He sends his tempest and throws me to the ground; quite without cause he inflicts on me many wounds. He will not even let me get my breath. Instead he fills me with bitterness' (9:17f.). 'Thou hast turned cruel to me, thou dost let me feel how much power thou hast' (30:21). Job believes and accepts that God is stronger; he is the Almighty. But does that mean that his God is necessarily in the right in his dispute with Job (9:19f.)? Now he has come to know this God as a God without love, without compassion for human beings in their misery, a God who despises all life on earth equally (9:32), since he has put power in the hands of scoundrels and blind judges (9:24). Finally Job resigns himself (9:28f.): he has to go on living with a God who oppresses him and whose anger is kindled against him. His cries for help are in vain (19:6-12).

Job demands an umpire who will arbitrate between the disputing parties, and administer justice. But this seems the most absurd demand of all, because the two parties are not equal and the weaker must always come off worse (9:32f.). God offers human beings no way out: 'If I now do wrong thou wilt not let it pass; if I succeed in something and feel proud, thou dost hunt me like a lion. . . . Thou hast never lack of witnesses against me, so that thou hast still more reason to harbour resentment against me, and to impose ever new penalties' (10:15-17). Since there is no independent authority which could set itself above him and his God and decide between them, Job hopes to be able to stand directly before his God and to receive from him the answer to his persistent questions (13:16).

In 19:23-29 Job implores his ransomer (go 'ēl), as his last hope; for only God himself can be this independent arbitrator who draws him out of his existential distress and crisis of faith. Crushed and robbed of all human dignity, Job expects the God he knows by faith (not from present experience) to take his part, maltreated as he is. Embittered, Job attacks his friends when they pose as God's spokesmen. To the degree in which they honestly try to find a theological explanation for Job's specific misfortunes, they are deceiving him and ultimately God too. Job still hopes that God will take him more seriously than his friends. With their theological training, they pursue knowledge at the expense of the individual sufferer: 'I could speak as you do, if you were in my place. I could wisely shake my head and lavish well-sounding phrases on you' (16:4; see also 13:7f.). Job's main question is really: What divine purpose lies behind my suffering? 'Is it his intention to torment me? Is he content when he can see that I am finished?' (16:7). Now that he has lost his friends, his health and his mental and spiritual balance, he is to be convicted of guilt as well! So, in his suffering, Job has come to know a God who is different from that God he has believed in hitherto. In the process his picture of God falls apart into two halves. He started off believing in the familiar (and calculable) God of his friends' theology. Now he encounters a hostile God who considers the standards of justice valueless. Job does not want to give up the God he has believed in; yet he is reluctantly compelled to recognise the God he has experienced in suffering. So he hopes, believes and demands that the God of his faith will vanquish and again supersede the violent and unjust God of his experience. He claims the restoration of the picture of God he had believed in.

(b) The Poem on Wisdom (28:1-28)

The poem on wisdom is a later interpolation and an extraneous element. The editor of the book put the poem into Job's mouth although its ideas in no way conform to Job's own. No answer is offered to the questions Job asks. On the contrary, this excursus on wisdom is an indication that no satisfactory answer can be given to these questions. Both the 'wisdom' discourse of the friends and Job's insistent questions are met by the pointer to the unfathomable element in creation which is within God's providence alone.

(c) The Elihu Speeches (32-37)

The arguments of the three friends seemed inadequate to the author of these speeches, while Job's accusations seemed to him presumptuous. So he tries in his composition to deepen the analysis of the situation and the answers proposed. He devotes a good deal of space to references to the Creator's greatness, almighty power and inscrutability (see especially 36:22-37:24). All human beings, even the mighty, are God's creatures; nothing is hidden from him. Moreover God is not as uninvolved as Job thinks: he speaks to people at night in dreams and visions; he sends sickness so that they may find their way back to him. Human beings cannot presume to judge God by their own standards of justice. God alone determines what is right. Only the person who has abandoned God would ever think of indicting him (36:13). Even if God allowed the distressful cries of the poor to go unheard, no one should condemn him for it (34:28f.). If he really remains silent, it is only because people are full of wickedness and pride (35:12). God purifies men and women through strokes of fate in order to teach them (36:8ff.). 'He who suffers will be improved through affliction. God opens his eyes through adversity' (36:15). Neither sin nor righteousness give or take anything away from God's power: 'He is not dependent on what you give him' (35:7). The doctrine of retribution is still in full force in Elihu's speeches (36:6ff.).

(d) God's Speeches and Job's Submission (38:1-42:6)

If our view of the history of the book's composition is correct, we may expect great things of God's own speeches, which are his final, decisive reply to Job's questions. What, in the author's view, has God himself to say about Job's problem? The reader may be disappointed to find that there is no neat, universally valid and mandatory theological solution at all. Job's questions are answered, not so much in the two long-winded discourses on God's almighty power,[7] as in Job's direct encounter with God. It is this confrontation which leads Job for the first time to humble submission, for 'I knew thee only from hearsay, but now my eye has seen thee' (42:5). Is this the end of all theology and any rational coming to terms with suffering and injustice? The author seems to suggest that only the personal encounter with God can bring the sufferer to the point of accepting his suffering in silence and resignation. All theological talk about suffering is hollow. It is true that God's own discourse is a theological one. But Job's capitulation is due, not to the arguments presented to him, but to the encounter with God itself. Only experience of the living God who enters into dialogue with the person involved, or instructs him personally, can convince Job.

3. SUMMING UP

There can surely be no doubt that the most striking thing about the Book of Job is its deliberately sustained pluralistic theology of suffering and justice. This suggests that one reason why the author of the poem embedded his dialogue in the already existing Job story was probably because he could then introduce more unobtrusively his daring attack on the God of classic, orthodox theology. The conclusion of the frame story (the restoration of Job to his former felicity) softens the whole; but it can never have been meant as more than a sop for pious ears. The author certainly did not intend to abandon the utterances made in the poem (see 42:7). The whole book is therefore an eloquent witness to the brittleness of traditional notions of faith and God. It makes it clear that the new theological approaches introduced here were gunpowder. The Book of Job shows a God who is far less concerned about the righteousness of the individual than the

God we find everywhere in prophetic literature. In God's own speeches Job is certainly urged to hold his tongue and stop attacking God; but he is not actually rebuked for these attacks on the traditional view of God (42:7). In the living God Job ultimately discovers his deliverer (*go 'ēl*) after all; and it is this deliverer who defends him against the crushing superiority and overpowering intransigence of the classic picture of God.

Translated by Margaret Kohl

Notes

1. For basic commentaries see the following: G. A. Driver and J. Gray *The Book of Job* International Critical Commentary 167 2nd ed. (Edinburgh 1950); G. Fohrer *Das Buch Hiob* Kommentar zum Alten Testament XVI (Gütersloh 1963); M. H. Pope *Job* The Anchor Bible (New York 1965); J. L'Évêque *Job et son Dieu. Essai d'exégèse et de théologie biblique* (Paris 1970); F. Horst *Hiob. Kapitel 1-19* Biblischer Kommentar XVI/17 3rd ed. (Neukirchen 1974); F. Hesse *Hiob*, Zürcher Bibelkommentar AT 14 (Zürich 1978).

2. When considering ancient Oriental parallels, special attention must be drawn to Babylonian, Egyptian and Ugaritic texts. See here D. Kinet 'Der Vorwurf an Gott' *Bibel und Kirche* 36 (1981) 259.

3. See here F. Hesse's critical comments in *Hiob*, cited in note 1, at p. 9f.

4. See the ideas about 'the sons of God' in the Ugaritic texts (fifteenth century B.C.). See D. Kinet *Ugarit. Geschichte und Kultur einer Stadt in der Umwelt des Alten Testaments* Stuttgarter Bibelstudien 104 (Stuttgart 1981) 136.

5. See here H. Haag *Teufelsglaube* (Tübingen 1974) p. 203f.

6. Zohpar's third discourse is, however, missing.

7. See the selection of negative judgments on the speeches of God in O. Keel *Jahwes Entgegnung an Ijob. Eine Deutung von Ijob 38-41 vor dem Hintergrund der zeitgenössischen Bildkunst* FRLANT 121 (Göttingen 1978) p. 11f.

PART III

Hope in another God

Jean Lévêque

Tradition and Betrayal
in the Speeches of the Friends

IT IS most tempting for interpreters of the Book of Job to highlight the tremendous faith of the principal character, to the extent that they denigrate the narrow minds and blind eyes of his three visitors, Eliphaz, Bildad and Zophar (chs. 4-27). In the dialogues of Job, however, the characters and the arguments are presented much more subtly, and their author could not be satisfied with contrasts that were superficial. He was writing during the first half of the fifth century, when a crisis in sapiential reflection was threatening to shake the very roots of the faith in Israel. The traditional teaching on the temporal retribution for both good and evil was proving to be useless as an explanation for the suffering of innocent people and therefore for some of the decisions made by God in his plans for mankind. Even before the Exile, the focal point of human and religious experience had been gradually moving away from the group towards the individual, and the feeling that there should be a new vision of man and of the world was constantly being reinforced in the zealous and cultured societies of Israel. The genius of the poet of Job lies in the way he accepts this shift of perspective—and all the insecurity entailed—yet attempts to write an original theological treatise on the destiny of man. By no means does he reject the traditional patterns of thought, inherited from several centuries of Jahwism: his work is in the form of a continuous dialogue between tradition—with the visitors acting as spokesmen—and the new questions on historical existence. This man's daring originality is coupled with a sincere respect for the laws of the past, and this is clearly evident, even in the way his work is presented: he has split the old prose narrative into two, using the Prologue and the Epilogue as flyleaves, retaining all their innocence, their optimism and their somewhat simplistic heroic splendour. It is within this classical framework that he has developed, at great length, his own vision of things, religious yet revolutionary. An examination into the origins of the images present in the dialogues between Job and his friends likewise shows that a surprising number of these have been borrowed from the following sources: the Israelite practice of judicial controversy, the psalms of complaint and, in more subtle fashion, the prophetic themes. In the Prologue Job is presented as a foreigner; in the dialogues, however, this passionate character conforms in thought and word to Israelite theology. Job is by no means disputing a faith which is foreign and inaccessible to him. Faith, distressing and unimpaired, is in fact the very reason behind his search for a new understanding of God and man.

Job's friends present him with the doctrine which, they say, conforms to tradition. We can only hope to understand Job's outbursts of indignation, abuse and despair by immediately specifying the way in which this doctrine is presented. The speeches of Eliphaz, Bildad and Zophar centre on three principal themes, which will be studied in turn: the punishment in store for the sinful, the bliss promised to the just, and man's unworthiness before God.

1. 'SUCH IS THE LOT OF THE WICKED MAN'

The theme of misfortune in store for the sinner is distributed fairly evenly throughout the speeches of all three friends. In the first cycle (chs. 4-14) it is only one argument among others and the death of the sinner is the most frequent topic of discussion; in the second cycle (chs. 15-21), as the punishment of the sinner is the only evidence used to support their argument, the visitors develop it at greater length; finally, in the last cycle (chs. 22-27), it is Zophar who tends to resume it.

There are times when the theme of the sinner's misfortune is linked with that of the happiness of the just. The distant origin of this combination is to be found in the sapiential reflection (e.g., Prov. 10-15) and in the conclusions to several 'instructions' in the diptych of the first set of the Proverbs (Prov. 2:21f.; 3:31ff.; 4:18f.). No typical example of this, however, is to be found in Job. When the punishment of the wicked is treated in large frescoes, it is in a way much closer to the psalmic tradition than to the Meshalim of the Sages. The closest literary genre to this is, in fact, the Complaint against the Enemies, which occurs frequently in the individual lamentations. The speeches in the Book of Job owe a great deal to this genre. To describe the conduct of the wicked, Eliphaz uses the psalmic image of wild beasts (4:10), and Bildad, the theme of the snare (18:8ff.). The arrogance of the enemies of God (15:25ff.) has likewise many parallels in the Psalms, and the cruelty of the mighty towards the poor is condemned in 20:20f., in the same way as in Psalms 10:8f.; 37:14f.; 94:5f.; and 109:16f., 20.

When describing the different modes of punishment, Job's friends tend to show a fondness for images evoking fragility and instability, insecurity and chagrin, anguish and despair. The images most favoured, however, are those concerning the path to extinction: the wicked man's home and lands are cursed, and brimstone is scattered upon them; his light is put out and everything pertaining to his happiness is destroyed; his food turns sour in his stomach (20:14; see Jeremiah 51:44); he perishes on the soil like a torn shoot and others sprout up in his place; he withers like a head of corn, attacked by drought from roots to foliage (18:16; see Amos 2:9). He is pushed from the light into the darkness; then comes a brutal death, as impious men are snatched away before their time (22:15f.). The sinner perishes for ever, like a ghost; he vanishes like a dream, like a vision of the night (Isaiah 29:7).

His punishment is not even over at death. Men for whom he cherished no affection soon forget that he ever existed. There is worse to come: his descendants are made to suffer. Those who survive him are buried by pestilence and he has no widows to mourn him. If he has many sons, it is for the sword, and his offspring go hungry; they are crushed in the gate, there is no one to deliver them, and they must repay the poor for the wrong their father has done. In the same way God punishes the cubs for the crimes of the lion, breaking off their fangs and scattering them. This idea of sons being punished for the sins of the father marks a movement away from the view taken in Ezekiel, namely that the individual is not responsible for the sins of family or clan.

Although they are not always explicit in attributing these chastisements to God, the three friends are absolutely convinced that he is always responsible. This is persistently stressed at critical points in the speeches. It does appear, however, that God is generally leaving it to secondary causes to effect punishment for breaches of the moral order. Everything happens as if God were freely choosing to guarantee a certain internal logic which produces misfortune in proportion to the fault: the wicked man 'stumbles in his own designs', 'reaps what he has sown', 'is father to what he has devised' (15:35; see Proverbs 14:22). The sinner, therefore, bears full responsibility for the punishment awarded and, according to Eliphaz, the foolish man kills himself through frustration and anger:

'Affliction does not come from the dust, nor does trouble sprout from the ground; but man engenders trouble as the sons of Réšef (eagles) fly upward' (5:2, 6f.).

The sentiments attributed to this avenging God are much less subtle than the ones he shows in the books of the prophets. There is a harshness, quite familiar to Job's visitors. God is not fooled, even when he is silent:

'He gives the wicked security and they are supported but his eyes are upon their ways.'

There comes a day when 'he who lays mighty hold on tyrants' rises; then, they 'despair of life' (24:22f.). God seems to have only one reaction at this point: anger. The wicked perish at the breath of his fury (see Psalm 90:7). Zophar even describes God in iron armour, relentlessly attacking his enemy (20:23ff.). It is true that the theme of the Warrior God appears in the Book of Job after a double literary transposition: it originally belonged to the epic songs of Israel (see Deuteronomy 32:40ff.) and it was often used by the psalmists to illustrate their certainty that the impious would be punished. Here, it is used in the psalmic tradition. This double re-use, however, does not totally overshadow the violence of the image.

Superficially classed among the sinners simply because he has fallen prey to misfortune, Job is expected to recognise in these long indictments his own condemnation. For the friends, misfortune means sin. Job vehemently challenges this argument, but from another point of view he still pays tribute to a certain theological archaism: he also sees his trials as a punishment, even if the fault is merely his opposition to the injustice of this punishment and the arbitrary nature which he attributes to God. He defies Eloah to tell him 'on what grounds he berates him', he reproves Eloah for fixing an imaginary guilt upon him, but he does not stop seeking a guilty party to explain the reason for his own distress. If it is not himself, it must be God.

2. 'AS A SHOCK OF GRAIN COMES UP TO THE THRESHING FLOOR IN ITS SEASON'

Happily, God's anger is not the only perspective which the friends offer to Job. There is a conflicting theme, also traditional, which emerges at intervals to counterbalance the excessive pictures of violence: the happiness in store for the just. It is developed at great length in the first cycle of speeches, makes no appearance at all in the second, and is only given about ten lines in the third (22:11-30). It would be illusive to say that the origin of this theme lies in the particular literary genre of religious blessings and promises of happiness: it forms part of the fund common to prophets, psalmists and sages, who are all mutually indebted to each other for images and expressions. In the books of prophecy, it is only rarely that the oracles of happiness are addressed to the individual: the joy that comes from God in response to conversion is meant to be shared by the whole nation. Both prophets and psalmists, however, stress that the true happiness—far exceeding all material gain—is to hope in Jahweh with a humble heart. Job's visitors, still faithful to the Israelite tradition, believe that there are four conditions for the believer's happiness:

D

(a) *Conversion.* Job must return to Shaddai, be reconciled and make peace with him (22:21ff.) and thus effect a return to morality. He will cast away the iniquity in his hand and he will not allow unrighteousness to dwell within his tent (11:14; 22:23). He will be delivered by the cleanness of his hands as he stands, true and perfect, before God (22:30). All this conforms to the teaching of the prophets.

(b) *Humility.* Eloah 'saves the lowly' (22:29).

(c) *Constancy of faith.* Once Job has returned to God he must 'set his heart aright' (11:13; see Psalm 78:8).

(d) *Prayer.* With regard to this, Job's friends have recourse to a precise—and heavily theological—terminology. They are not urging Job towards a third-rate spiritual experience. Bildad first of all suggests that he should 'seek' God (*sĭhér*). This is the verb used by the sages to express the constant search for wisdom. In Psalm 78:34 it is used with regard to conversion. It concerns a search for God which consumes the whole being, moving the believer to the point of anguish (Hosea 5:15). Isaiah simultaneously associates with it the concepts of expectation, desire and memory (Isaiah 26:8f.). Moreover, the prayer of Job is to become one of entreaty and supplication (8:5), like the distressed call of the conquered (1 Kings 8:33), the exiled, the accused (Job 9:15) or those in fear for their lives (Genesis 42:21; Hosea 12:5). It is a passionate supplication which can be expressed in cries before God (Psalms 30:9; 142:2). Job will make his to God by stretching out his cleansed hands to him (11:13).

Given the theory that Job is a sinner, this advice—which can in no way be attacked on theological grounds—combines both the soundest intuitions and the most authentic attitudes belonging to Israelite spirituality. For Job, the drama is not that his friends are speaking falsely but that their words are perverted by their interpretation of his suffering. The assumption that the man tried is the man chastised means that one is debarred from saying even one word, either about God or to the sufferer.

In their descriptions of happiness itself—and not merely the conditions for this happiness—the three visitors often find it more difficult to separate the theological from the utilitarian. Conforming to tradition, they present the just man as serene and immune to all misfortune. They promise him a sound enjoyment of life and a success exceeding the domestic situation. After a fruitful and harmonious life, Job will go to the grave at a ripe old age 'as a shock of grain comes up to the threshing floor in its season' (5:26). But to effect this happiness, his relationship with God must flourish. God will tirelessly watch over Job, and redeem him as he always redeems the innocent; with healing hands he himself will tend the wounds of his faithful servant. Job, 're-established in his house of justice' will lift up to God a face without blemish (11:15); his prayer will be answered and, filled with the goodness of Eloah, he will pay his vows. Then he will be able to 'lay gold in the dust' (22:24) in comparison to the joy he will find in God. Shaddai will be for him his 'gold and precious silver'. One sentence uttered by Eliphaz admirably sums up the new intimacy that the converted Job could have in God: 'Then you will delight yourself in Shaddai' (22, 26). This verb is one of the favourite words used in the Isaian tradition to express spiritual joy and its impact on man (Isaiah 55:2f.; 58:13; 66:11; see Psalms 37:4, 11).

To be honest, the friends do not always keep to this level of perspective, and the idea of bargaining with God is unpleasantly prominent in several parts of the text: 'Agree with God and be at peace; thereby good will come to you' (22:21). These interested designs threaten to hold faith in check, and in the end Job's visitors are unable to dissociate the relationship with God from all insurance policies against fate. Once again we can appreciate the weight that the axiom of temporal retribution carried in Israelite theology.

We have to steer clear of all anachronism in this area. A voluntary historical displacement is necessary if the theologian versed in Christian eschatology is to understand the concept of a life with God vanishing at the gates of death. Lack of this intellectual asceticism meant that many of the reactions and new endeavours of the sages of Israel could be abruptly dismissed as the incoherent babbling of an immature theology; it would, in fact, have been beneficial to examine the theocentric philosophy of these sages, and the riches inherent in their love of life and their paradoxical hope.

As regards Job's visitors, one can only be struck at the way they insist on being heard before being discredited. Their *a priori* assertion of Job's guilt undoubtedly closes their minds to the true theological dimensions of the mystery of his suffering; these particular points—their ill-knowledge of the man and their interpretation of his trials—could form the entire subject matter for a critique of the friends and their language. Much of their affirmation, however, would be easily countersigned by prophets and psalmists. They put emphasis on a spiritual tradition which would be valid in other contexts; often what they do wrong is right from their point of view. This is particularly so with regard to their third argument: the radical unworthiness of man before God.

3. 'WHAT IS MAN THAT HE CAN BE CLEAN?'

The theme of the unworthiness of man recurs twice in the speeches of Eliphaz (4:17-21; 15:14ff.) and only once in those of Bilbad (25:4ff.). A study of these three texts reveal three constant features:

(*a*) The theme is always presented in the form of a double question. 'Can mortal man be righteous before God?' 'Can a man be pure before his maker?' (4:17; see 15:14; 20:4).

(*b*) The exposition of the theme is always followed by an *a fortiori* argument. God convicts his angels of deviation; he does not have faith even in his saints; the stars are not pure to his eyes. How then can he be expected to find any moral integrity in the man who 'dwells in a house of clay'?

(*c*) The three texts put into parallel the themes of justice ($s^e d\bar{a}q\bar{a}h$) and moral purity (*thr, zkh*).

In the Old Testament, it is often in contrast to God's power and sanctity that man becomes aware of his own unworthiness (Isaiah 6:1-6). 'Jahweh, who is like you?' is the cry of the Psalmists (Psalms 89:7ff.; 76:8; 113:5; see 1 Samuel 2:2). This theme of the creator's inaccessible majesty appears frequently in the psalms and it is readily used by the sages to support their theory of retribution. In Psalms 143:2 and 130:3, the faithful man pleads his own unworthiness as a preventative measure against an over-harsh chastisement (see 1 Kings 8:46; Amos 7:2, 5; Proverbs 20:9; Psalms 19:13; Ecclesiastes 7:20). It is obvious from all these texts that in Old Testament mentality man's weakness is seen as an excuse for his sins and as a means for drawing upon God's mercy. The three friends, by distorting this theme, will use it as a weapon against Job.

Their reasoning is simple. Man has no valid argument to make and, above all, no right to justify himself before God—his very limitations forbid it. Not that engendering and birth essentially mean blemish, for if man 'is born of woman' (*y^e l\bar{u}d 'iššāh*), this expression denotes nothing other than caducity. According to Job's friends, however, this caducity is undoubtedly an indication of moral conduct: a weak body means a labile will. Here Job's accusers are merely following a tradition marked by Psalms 39, 78, 90 and 103, by Ecclesiasticus 17:30ff. and by the Hōdayōt of Qumran (12:24-31; 13:15). The themes of human caducity and sin—quite distinct theologically—often come close together in the texts, and a verse in Job (15:14ff.) is a typical example of this: man is first described, inoffensively, as 'born of woman', yet two lines later he becomes 'one who is abominable and corrupt, a man who drinks iniquity like water'. The severity of the friends, however, is actually contrary to tradition. Job, in 14:1-4, refers to man's inevitable impurity as an extenuating circumstance that God should take into consideration. Eliphaz's reply is cutting and permits no hope: man has no excuse, for it is his wilful malignity that makes him abominable in God's eyes.

Although they concern either the retribution of just and wicked, or the no less traditional motif of human limitations, the arguments of Job's visitors, therefore, only serve to stress and illustrate the same fundamental misunderstanding. Job acknowledges his own—and every man's—finite nature, and he willingly adds to the assertions of his friends on this point; he refuses, however, to accept an alleged culpability as the reason behind his suffering. His preachers speak to him about transgression—at the very moment when he feels himself the object of God's aggression. He suffers, and yet he has always sought God. It cannot thus be true that happiness is always the consequence of goodness; his unmerited misfortunes can only be attributed to God, who has 'turned cruel' to him (30:21). What is the meaning of these sufferings, what is the true face of God? For Job, these two questions are now related, and it is to God that he intends to address them.

The visitors believe that they already have the answer, and find its elements in tradition—as they interpret it. It is true that they invent nothing new, and they are not responsible for the problems of this tradition. Their mistake lies in obscuring these problems to safeguard—at all costs—the security of a system. Moreover, in the very way that they conform to tradition, they betray the message by betraying the friendship: to use the Word of God against man to humiliate or silence him is to falsify the Word of God—always. 'Maxims of ash!' is Job's retort to them, and he resolutely turns his back upon this false revival of the certitudes of faith.

Beyond this fruitless dialogue with his friends, Job paradoxically pursues his dialogue with the Absent One and, standing alone, he persists in demanding a confrontation which he both desires and dreads. He has faithfully preserved his relationship with God; he therefore has the right to defend it. But his defence of self means that he is trying to outdo God. Can a man assert his own integrity, his own justice if he has to assert it against the Creator? It is there that the whole drama of Job lies, at a depth inaccessible to learned verbosity, in the conflict between his relationship with God and his relationship with himself.

Luis Alonso-Schökel

God's Answer to Job

IN DRAMATIC terms, God has to speak in order to answer, from a position of superiority or supremacy, the case of the four friends, since they have used God in their argument and his prestige is therefore at stake. In dramatic terms, again, God has to speak because Job has challenged him to a verbal duel. At this stage it is impossible for God to be neutral: if he does not intervene, the thesis of the four friends will be discredited, since it will mean that God can be accused with impunity. And Job will be the winner, since he has left God speechless. The dynamics of the poem require that God should intervene. Both actors and audience expect it of him. The content of his intervention has proved disconcerting to not a few readers and to many commentators.

We may select a few of the opinions expressed. Its literary excellence is praised: 'the crown and climax of the book' (E. Sellin); 'marvellous images expressed in marvellous words' (D. B. Macdonald). At the same time its inappropriateness is condemned: 'magnificent impertinence' (C. J. Ball); 'pezzi di bravura' (D. H. Duesberg); 'this beautiful nature poem could not heal a sick heart' (P. Volz); 'like shaking a rattle at a crying child to divert its attention from hunger' (R. A. F. McKenzie), etc. The fact is that the commentator's judgment depends on his *expectation* of what will happen when God intervenes: if a person feels cheated, it is because he was expecting something different. Not only the critic's judgment, but also his treatment of the text, depend on his expectations: for example, the discovery of glosses, or the excision of supposedly spurious passages, or the selection of relevant details, and so on.

We cannot read these speeches without bringing to them some kind of expectation; but we must not judge them without taking account of the expectation factor, which conditions us as we read and as we form our judgment.

What are the *friends* expecting? In response to Job's audacious challenge, they are expecting a thunderbolt to strike him and finally reduce him to silence. Such is the implication of their theory of retribution:

> To fill his belly to the full
>   God will send his fierce anger into him,
>   and rain it upon him in his flesh. . . . (20:23)
> Utter darkness is laid up for his treasures;
>   a fire not blown upon will devour him. . . . (20:26)
> The heavens will reveal his iniquity,
>   and the earth will rise up against him (20:27).

In the view of his friends, torn between compassion and satisfaction, Job's end will surely be torment.

Job himself is looking for a dramatic encounter, a dialogue in which both parties will have an equal right to present their arguments, and for a final declaration of his own innocence and God's guilt.

What is the *audience*, or the *reader*, expecting? An intellectual response to a problem of theology or theodicy? Compassion and understanding for the innocent sufferer? Between Job and his friends, the reader will have chosen to take the side of the hero, since the development of the poem demands it, since this is the way the author has been conditioning his reader. But between God and Job, will the reader have taken the man's side, like Job's wife, or God's side, because that is the way it should be? Perhaps his expectation will be ambiguous.

We can distinguish two types of expectation: one closed, the other open. Closed expectation digs out a channel in advance, and refuses to accept any dénouement which follows a different channel. Open expectation looks in a particular direction, but is prepared to do a detour in order to follow the way out suggested by the text. In the first type of expectation, because the author's final response (through the mouth of one of his characters) does not fit in with my preconceptions, I either reject it, or criticise it, or select what I want from it. In the second type of expectation, although the author chooses a route I was not expecting and so at first disorientates me, I nevertheless try to follow him and discover where his trail is leading.

This has not been a digression, but is rather a critique of over-hasty criticism. It was necessary to establish our frame of mind before turning the page and reading God's intervention. In it, after the impassioned dialogue about justice, God ranges over a whole cosmic series which includes earth and sea, the dawn, meteors, constellations, wild animals, and descriptions of two half-real, half-fantastic creatures. Is God answering the problem under discussion? Is he answering the characters in the drama?

He is answering the *friends* indirectly. They stood by the doctrine of retribution, on the basis of which they argued: Job is suffering, so he must be guilty. Even if no guilt attached to his former actions, it certainly does to his more recent words. He deserves to be punished for them. But he has a way of escape: he can confess his sin, ask for forgiveness, and amend his ways. In his reply, God takes no account of the friends' main thesis. He neither proclaims nor endorses the doctrine of retribution. He does not condemn Job.

Job was asking for several things, or a single thing expressed in different ways.

(*a*) He wanted to *meet God*:

> . . . yet I will defend my ways to his face.
> This will be my salvation,
>   that a godless man shall not come before him (13:15f.)
> Oh, that I knew where I might find him,
>   that I might come even to his seat (23:3).

So then, God reveals himself in the whirlwind and Job recognises the fact: 'now my eye sees thee' (42:5). Job obtains the meeting he has sought, he finds himself with God. There is a resemblance here to Psalm 73, which clearly lies behind the book. The psalmist was facing a two-sided problem, which was part of his own experience: the prosperity of the wicked, and the suffering of the upright. He has been in danger of collapse, he has tried to resolve the problem by dint of reflection, but has been compelled to admit failure. At that moment God invites him to come up to his own lofty viewpoint, so that he may see from a distance the fate of the wicked, and above all invites him to share the incomparable, ineffable presence of God: 'for me it is good to be near God'. We may recall too the vision of Jacob in Genesis 32: the patriarch comes out of his struggle limping, but content, 'because I have seen God face to face, and yet my life is preserved'. Since the vision of God can be fatal to man, the fact that Job has seen God and remained alive is in itself an important justification of him.

(b) But the theophany and the vision that goes with it are not the whole story. Job wanted to have a dialogue, to enter into *discussion with God*. There is traditionally a link between theophany and word (see Exod. 20:20; Ps. 50:3, 7, 21). The hero's desire and prayer are expressed in the following verses:

> Only grant two things to me,
>   then I will not hide myself from thy face:
> withdraw thy hand far from me,
>   and let not dread of thee terrify me.
> Then call, and I will answer;
>   or let me speak, and do thou reply to me.
> How many are my iniquities and my sins?
>   Make me know my transgression and my sin.
> Why dost thou hide thy face,
>   and count me as an enemy? (13:20-24).

Job, tired of the conventional and inconclusive arguments of his friends, wanted to enter into a direct dialogue with God. This is granted to him. Job had generously offered his rival the choice as to where they would meet and who would speak first. God agrees to speak, and put questions to Job. His discourse meets honourably the expectations of Job. With his impassioned words, with his challenge, Job has succeeded in getting God to speak: could there be a greater triumph?

The theme of accusation had come into Job's challenge: 'How many are my iniquities and my sins?' God does not reply directly to this, and his silence is eloquent. Does he thereby cheat Job's expectation? In no way. By remaining silent on this point, God recognises the validity of Job's protestation of innocence and the falsity of the imputations of his friends. 'As God lives, who has taken away my right . . ., I hold fast my righteousness, and will not let it go' (27:2, 6). By his silence God confirms Job's innocence and does not retract the favourable judgment pronounced in the prologue of the book: 'blameless and upright, one who feared God, and turned away from evil'. Job is reproached only for criticising God's plan without understanding it.

(c) Job was asking for some *respite* from his suffering before he died, and that hostilities should cease:

> Let me alone, that I may find a little comfort (10:20; see ch. 16).

In this, Job is largely successful. His cosmic tour under God's guidance is a respite from pain rather than an occasion of happiness. The ironical and condescending tone used by God shows that there is no hostility. Job feels that he is inwardly reconciled with God, though he smarts under the questions. God speaks no explicit words of comfort, though his tone is persuasive and has the power to bring peace, and that is enough. God is not a 'treacherous torrent-bed' (6:15), like the friends. Here is an understanding firmness, which reminds us of a father: 'he knows our frame; he remembers that we are dust' (Ps. 103:14). The blessed respite will give way to a stage of full and generous restoration.

(d) From his friends, Job was looking for loyalty, *understanding*, persuasive words:

'He who withholds kindness from a friend
    forsakes the fear of the Almighty' (6:14)
'Teach me, and I will be silent;
    make me understand how I have erred.
How forceful are honest words!
But what does reproof from you reprove?' (6:24f.).

What he failed to find in his friends, Job has found in God. In the midst of reproaches he has found compassion, understanding, persuasive arguments. Except that what convinces Job may not convince a section of the audience. They will object that the author affirms the persuasive value of the divine discourse, but does not succeed in communicating the persuasion directly to the reader. That is to say, the discourse is persuasive for the author, persuasive for the character Job, but not so for the intelligent and critical reader. Is this the case?

(e) Finally, as a corollary of his own innocence, Job was wanting to demonstrate the *guilt of his rival*. God would be unjust if he ill-treated his servant 'without cause'. Does Job attain this last objective? It is to be noted that he does not seek this for its own sake, but as the necessary correlative of his own innocence. Does God respond in any way to this element of correlativity?

We already possess most of the data. Now we must concentrate our attention on God's response. Does God accept, discuss, or resolve the central question of his justice in relation to the person who suffers? Or does he skilfully avoid it? A number of commentators deplore the disappearance of ethics into aesthetics. In the words of E. Bloch: 'he answers moral problems with physical problems'.

To find an answer to the question, I am going to look again at the arguments of Job (following, in part, O. Keel). Job suffers, knowing himself to be innocent. It therefore follows that God is treating him unjustly. And he is not an exception, since God either makes no distinction between good people and bad, or in fact favours the bad, or takes no interest in the world, with the result that injustice holds the upper hand. In such a situation, it would be better if the world were to return to chaos (ch. 3). For Job, his own undeserved suffering, the ethical disorder in the world, and the forces of chaos, all hang together. His starting-point is his own experience. His conclusion must be God.

God accepts the question, and in part Job's statement of it, and makes a number of affirmations: that he has a plan or design (38:2), that the existence of evil and injustice forms part of this plan (40:11f.), that he constantly exercises control and dominion over the forces of evil and chaos. God does this by arguing directly with Job, and proving by analogy or symbolically his complete dominion. It is by no means certain that these chapters will have nothing to do with the problem of justice. To begin with, we must remember that in the Old Testament justice is traditionally linked with wisdom. This idea finds its fullest expression in the Book of Wisdom, which sees knowledge or prudence as the basis of just government. In Job, justice is expressly spoken of in connection with the cosmic theme of the morning (38:13), and is implied in the reference to battle (38:23). God tackles directly the fundamental question of the correlation of innocence and guilt (40:7-14), and opposes Job's acute statement of the problem. This occurs in the middle of the divine discourse, after Job's first confession, and has the tone of a passionate appeal. Finally God turns to justice and expounds symbolically the power of evil and the basic or daily victory over it. Among the symbols, there stands out one which Job can understand perfectly, since he himself has made use of it: the symbol of light and darkness. To this may be added another classical symbol—that of stability and turbulence. The two animals of the final part are symbols of chaotic power.

Now let us turn to the heart of the discourse, and read it again:

'Then the Lord answered Job out of the whirlwind:
"Gird up your loins like a man;
    I will question you, and you declare to me.
Will you even put me in the wrong?
    Will you condemn me that you may be justified?
Have you an arm like God,
    and can you thunder with a voice like his?
Deck yourself with majesty and dignity;
    clothe yourself with glory and splendour.
Pour forth the overflowings of your anger,
    and look on every one that is proud, and abase him.
Look on every one that is proud, and bring him low;
    and tread down the wicked where they stand.
Hide them all in the dust together;
    bind their faces in the world below.
Then will I also acknowledge to you,
    that your own right hand can give you victory" ' (40:6-14).

In the second volume of his enormous commentary, Pineda wrote, in explanation of verse 8:

'In protesting his innocence, afflicted without reason, Job seemed to be bringing a charge of injustice against the judge who punished without reason' (p. 1020, 2).

'Although in the judgment you may protest your righteousness and innocence, and although I may absolve you publicly of any suspicion of sin, you will not on that account be able to accuse me of any sin' (p. 1024, 5).

This second volume dates from 1602. Pineda is right in saying that the innocence claimed by Job neither implies nor requires the guilt of God. He is wrong to the extent that he cannot rid himself of the concept of God as judge, and does not recognise the concept of God as one of the parties in a legal action—which is how the hero himself sees it. Once we introduce the notion of two opposing sides in a legal argument, the text will be illuminated for us. Such a legal action presupposes a previous obligation, natural or positive, between the parties. The party who considers himself offended serves a summons on the other and goes to law with him, with a view to obtaining a confession and the satisfaction due to him. Since the two parties are correlative parts of a law-suit, the innocence of one implies the guilt of the other. I quote some examples from the Old Testament:

'The Lord is in the right, and I and my people are in the wrong' (Exod. 9:27—Pharaoh is speaking).
'You are righteous and not I' (1 Sam. 24:17—Saul is speaking to David).
'Thou art justified in thy sentence, and blameless in thy judgment' (Psalm 51:4).

(This theme is developed in my book *Treinta Salmos. Poesía y Oración*, in the commentary on Psalms 50 and 51.)

One party must be condemned, in order that the other may be acquitted. Job knows himself to be innocent, and therefore God must be guilty. God does not contest the first part: when Job was not listening, God pronounced him just; in answering him, he lays no blame upon him. What God rejects is the formulation:

man must be condemned in order that God may be justified;
God must be condemned in order that man may be justified.

Is it true that there is no way out of the dilemma? For the moment a simple negative must suffice: it is more important to reject the formulation than to accept an answer to any of its parts, because the formulation determines the problem and its solution. So much for verse 8.

When we turn to verses 9-14—Job's theophany, and God's hymn of praise to him—it is necessary to establish a point which is not explicit. In this kind of legal contest, two persons or groups are involved. What happens if a third party is introduced? Let us suppose that X suffers because of Y, and Z either acquiesces in or tolerates the injustice. Z is then unjust towards X by dint of tolerating Y. Jeremiah puts it well in one of his impassioned confessions: 'Do not by your patience let me perish' (15:15). Jeremiah has fulfilled his obligations to God. God does not fulfil his obligations to Jeremiah, since, by treating the prophet's persecutors with indulgence, he causes the innocent to suffer. (The verse quoted should be read in the context of the whole series of confessions in 15:10-21 and 20:7-18. The second of these passages has influenced the Book of Job.)

Thus the horizon of Job is widened by the inclusion of a third party in the reckoning—the wicked people mentioned, or alluded to, or symbolised, in the previous chapters, and also Satan in the narrative prologue. What can a just sovereign do with an evil power? Perhaps make an end of it, as Ps. 101:8 suggests: 'cutting of all the evildoers from the city of the Lord', or as Jeremiah himself prayed: 'Pull them out like sheep for the slaughter, and set them apart for the day of slaughter' (12:3). Something of the kind is suggested by God to Job: that he should take over the reins of the world, appear in a theophany and annihilate the wicked. Would this be the solution? Would it be a real victory? St Augustine writes in his commentary on Psalm 122:

'He is righteous before God. He is rich. His heart is full of righteousness, since it seems to him that God is doing his work badly, and he thinks that he himself is righteous. And if you were to allow him to steer the ship, he would wreck it. He wants to oust God from control of the world, and himself take the helm of creation, allotting sorrows and joys, punishments and rewards, to all. Poor man!' (CCSL XL, 1823).

What is interesting in this passage is the linking together of the sense of justice, the accusing of God, and the control of the world. Indeed God does not destroy harmful animals, he will not destroy Behemoth and Leviathan, he has not destroyed Satan. Will Job presume to do it? Would it be possible? Would he be any the better for it?

In verse 14 God's irony reaches its limit. The second half of the verse is an adapted quotation from Psalm 98:1b; 'his right hand . . . (has) gotten him the victory'. This psalm belongs to the spiritual world of Deutero-Isaiah, with its emphasis on the regal dignity of God. It speaks of a historic victory with which God inaugurates a new age: 'he will judge the world with righteousness'. In Job 40:14, the roles are reversed: Job will play God, and God will sing him a hymn of praise.

This passage calls for reflection. Job's implicit statement of the case was: one party must be condemned so that the other may be acquitted. This formulation, rejected by God, reappears in various forms.

On one side there are those who pass easy judgment on other people's misfortunes: 'It was God's punishment!' They imagine that they do justice to God by thinking and speaking of him as a merciless despot, quick to exact retribution. Their God is a God without compassion, and they see life and history as ruled by almost mechanical ethical laws. God is for them a factor to be used in explaining to men, by an ethical reasoning-process, calamitous events. The representative of this school or attitude pronounces a religious judgment in which, at one and the same time, man is condemned and God is justified.

On the other side there are those who try to condemn God in order to justify man.

They condemn God perhaps to non-existence, because they think he humiliates man, deprives him of his freedom, distracts him and takes him away from his temporal tasks. Or they condemn God for inaction, because he does not immediately intervene on the side of justice, because he makes, or allows, the innocent to suffer. . . .

Although the approach which we may call 'judicial' may be applicable in certain cases, it is unjust both to God and man if it is taken as a general principle, and in particular cases it has to be applied with caution. Is it satisfactory to say that the concept of mutual rights is the only possible way of understanding even human relations? And in our relations with God are there not other concepts to be taken into account, such as praise, trust and love?

In the baptism of Jesus, the Father declares the complete innocence of his Son. Satan drives Judas to betray Jesus, who thus undergoes the supreme test of innocent suffering. Accused and condemned before the human political and religious tribunal, Jesus is rehabilitated by his Father, and he prays for those who cause his suffering. The pattern is not totally dissimilar from that of Job. How does Jesus Christ approach the Father?

St Paul teaches us that, if a man insists on the approach I have called judicial, he stands only to lose. Because, as the Book of Job says, man cannot argue against God, and because his reasoning and his rights would be based on services rendered and laws obeyed. Paul insists as strongly as he can on the concepts of grace and faith in our relations with the God and Father of Jesus Christ.

Translated by G. W. S. Knowles

Bibliography

Alonso-Schökel, L. and Sicre Diaz, J. L. *Sapienciales. Comentario: II Job* (Madrid 1983) (on which this article has been based).

Dhorme, P. *Le Livre de Job* (Paris 1926); *A Commentary on the Book of Job* (London 1967).

Glatzer, N. N. *The Dimensions of Job* (New York 1969) (a collection of essays by various authors).

Gordis, R. *The Book of Job* (New York 1978).

Horst, F. *Hiob (1-19)* (Neukirchen 1960-1968).

Keel, O. *Jahwes Entgegnung an Job* (Göttingen 1978).

Kuhl, C. *Theologische Rundschau 21* (1953) pp. 163-205; 267-317; *Theologische Rundschau 22* (1954) pp. 261-316 (with full bibliographical information).

Lévêque, J. *Job et son Dieu* (Paris 1970).

Pineda, J. *In Job libri tredecim* (Madrid 1595, 1601).

Ravasi, G. *Giobbe* (Rome 1979).

Sanders, P. S. *Twentieth Century Interpretations of the Book of Job* (Englewood Cliffs N.J. 1968).

Schultens, A. *Liber Iobi cum nova versione ad Hebraeum fontem et commentario perpetuo* (Leiden 1737).

Terrien, S. and Scherer, P. *The Book of Job* (1954); *Job* (Neuchâtel 1963) (in French).

Jean-Claude Sagne

The Cry of Jesus on the Cross

IT IS through the cry of Jesus that we can understand the spiritual drama of Job. The passion of Jesus and its presence in the Church come between the sufferer of the time of the first alliance and ourselves. The glory of the cross provides the only light by which we can apprehend Job's ordeal. That at any rate is the way opened up to us by a spiritual reading of the sacred scriptures, the central principle of which is the accomplishment by Jesus of all the figures of the Old Testament.

We shall, therefore, begin by seeking to understand something of the cry of Jesus on the cross before returning to the spiritual drama of Job. But what is the relationship between what Jesus suffered in his passion and what Job discovered in his ordeal? The upshot of our reflection will be to suggest that the spiritual suffering of Jesus consists not in the repetition of the interior ordeal of Job but in its transposition to an altogether deeper plane and in a response to it in the form of a testimony. It is also possible to see in the passion of Jesus a sort of realisation of what Job prefigured, but such a realisation is a spiritual accomplishment rather than a literal reproduction written somewhat larger. This is why it is the passion of Jesus that must be the starting-point of our reading of Job, for the 'language of the cross' (1 Cor. 1:18) is the supreme wisdom in all that touches the destiny of man in his relationship to God.

Our reflection will, therefore, proceed in two stages: by way of (1) a meditation on Jesus' cry on the cross; and (2) an interpretation of the suffering Job's protest. I shall end with the spirituality of the cross, suggesting the value of the cross as a recapitulation and accomplishment of all spiritual suffering.

1. THE CRY OF JESUS ON THE CROSS

'Now from the sixth hour there was darkness over all the land until the ninth hour. And about the ninth hour Jesus cried with a loud voice, "Eli, Eli, lama sabacthani?" that is, "My God, my God, why hast thou forsaken me?" ' (Matt. 27:45-46).

The cry of Jesus consists in the citation of verse 2 of psalm 21. It upsets the delicate balance to take this verse away from the whole psalm of which it is the introduction and the threshold, but it upsets even more to cancel out the import of this cry by reassuringly emphasising the note of praise with which the psalm ends. The fact is that this psalm is a song of deliverance which glorifies the Lord for having saved the poor man from his attackers. What we have to do is to take the psalm as a whole as a horizon of confidence and praise against which a cry that is nevertheless intolerable stands out.

52

'My God, my God, why hast thou forsaken me?' After the repetition of the opening invocation, which serves to reinforce its supplicatory power, the question thrown out by Jesus is not so much a request for an explanation as a searing lucidity about his entire dereliction. It is a cry of loneliness. There is a well-known fragment from Pascal's *Pensées* that is relevant here: '. . . Jesus is alone on the earth, not only in feeling and sharing his pain, but in knowing it: only he and heaven know it. . . . He suffers this pain in the abandonment and the horror of night. I think that Jesus complained only this once, but he then does so as if he could no longer contain an impossible suffering.'[1] Jesus suffers from being abandoned by everyone, even by his God and Father.

How does the Father abandon his Son in the hour of his passion? How does Jesus feel himself abandoned by the Father? There is first of all the silence of God in the face of the insults and blasphemies that are hurled at the Son and discredit him as the false Messiah. There is also the apparent passivity of God in regard to the torture inflicted on the man of sorrows, the suffering servant. God seems to have withdrawn entirely from the scene of judgment. He allows the innocent man to be accused, condemned and executed.

That, however, is not all. Beyond the religious and political proceedings that end in eliminating a Messiah who dashes the expectations of the Jewish crowd and those who manipulate it, there is about the passion of Jesus a much more mysterious and impalpable dimension which is that of a spiritual combat with Satan and all the powers of darkness. Before trying to decipher this unseen warfare I should like to say from the outset that we can bear the light on this subject only in so far as we cleave, with a faith that lives in love and prayer, to the perfect and constant communion of the Son and the Father in that ocean of peace which is the divine life. For the rest, it is the gradual and always very partial discovery of the depths of Trinitarian life which gives us an inkling of the gravity and intensity of the spiritual combat of the cross. As soon as one begins to leave aside, let alone to misunderstand, the permanence of the perfect union of the Son with the Father to whom he does not cease to return in obedience and adoration, attention to the cross becomes intolerable and gives rise to various contradictions. The cross can be thought of tragically or it can be idealised, but either way one inevitably ends up with the same paradoxical and yet understandable conclusion, namely, the relativisation of the place of the cross in the life of a Christian.

Now the cry of Jesus on the cross seems to lend itself to a tragic reading of the scene of Calvary: the Father's unleashing of his anger against the innocent victim in whom he ceases to recognise his beloved Son is a breach of the communion of the Trinity. And as for idealising the cross, this consists in so emphasising the unique value of the sacrifice of Jesus that its perfection makes the attempt of the disciple to imitate it not only useless but misplaced. What is astonishing in the discovery of the mystery of the cross at the centre of the Christian life is that the more its inescapable presence is accepted, the more it absorbs tendencies towards a doloristic or masochistic sensibility, without ever doing away with them entirely. It is keeping the cross at a distance that secretes idealised or terrifying notions of it which then justify and perpetuate themselves. That is why we have to keep on starting time and again from what constitutes the deepest reality of the event of the cross: the love of Jesus for the Father. It is just this immeasurable love of the incarnate Son who wants to return to his Father with everything he has that enables us to get a glimpse of the spiritual combat which he undergoes and also to hear and understand his cry of dereliction.

The mystery of the incarnate Lord is that he recapitulates in himself the whole of human history seen as a holy history, that is to say, as a response to the invitations of God. This recapitulation is above all in the order of love. Jesus in his humanity is inhabited by a love for the Father that is so simple, complete and full that he draws everything he carries within himself towards the Father in his wake, and this includes not only his own human nature but that of each one of us too. This is obviously not a question of supposing that Jesus lives out an offering of love for the Father in the place of each one of us by way of substituting for our personal life. The role of Jesus is more that of witness and guide. He concentrates within himself everything that can illumine and direct men's return to the Father by way of filial confidence and abandonment to the will of the Father. That is why Jesus in the time of his agony and passion endures all the spiritual ordeals that can affect man in his return to God. It is to the extent that he carries them within himself that he can by his living presence today help us to bear and to surmount them. To sum up, Jesus' love for the Father is that of an elder brother concerned to open up the road to the younger ones who follow him in trust. This is why Jesus takes on the heaviness of the burden that most weighs down sinful man's élan towards his creator and father.

This is where I should like to place the spiritual context of the conflict between sinful man and God who calls him. What the epistle to the Hebrews stresses above all is the spiritual obstacle represented by the fear of death, a fear that is in fact the source, prototype and ultimate figure of all human anguish. It is by way of this fear of death that he who enslaves man by holding the power of death and playing on it becomes discernible: 'Since therefore the children share in flesh and blood, he himself likewise partook of the same nature, that through death he might destroy him who has the power of death, that is, the devil, and deliver all those who through fear of death were subject to lifelong bondage' (Heb. 2:14-15). The fear of death is one of the typical consequences of original sin. At its most intense this fear can include the fear of death which is the reaction of the guilty man. Fear of God, fear of being punished and abandoned by him, of losing one's life, is the fate of a man who lets himself be shut up in his sin. Jesus as the beloved Son of the Father comes to reestablish trust in the goodness, sweetness and mercy of the Father.

But the drama in question goes much further than the struggle against the anguish of death that can assail every man. Jesus is in the grip of the one who holds the power of death, the father of lies and killing. In the course of his agony and passion Jesus is attacked by the Adversary, he who wishes to prevent the deliverance of the human race which he holds captive, especially by means of distorted notions of God. The cry of Jesus on the cross is therefore to be understood as the ultimate expression of the spiritual darkness of one who finds himself overwhelmed by an evil that is more serious, obscure and fearful than the violence of men. It is the cry of the innocent man encircled by lying and orchestrated accusations. It is the cry of a man who sees his death to be very close and inescapable. Beyond even that it is the cry of somebody who feels himself oppressed by a superhuman hand inflicting an interior torment which is of a different order from the convulsion of anguish occasioned by a merely psychic crisis.

At the same time this cry remains a prayer and its very intensity is an appeal to God. It is to the Father that Jesus speaks in order to address him as 'My God'. We need a lot of trust and love in order to be able to share with those nearest us what troubles us most, especially in our relationship to them. It is also because Jesus has such complete filial trust in the Father that he experiences so painfully the feelings and thoughts of revolt and sadness that can shoot through him in his sharing of the spiritual combat of the sinful man. Jesus' greatest suffering in his passion is to undergo the interior temptation to despair of his mission to save, because what he offers man as a proof of the redemptive love and mercy of the Father, the gift of his life as the Good Shepherd, becomes the place where men unleash their violence and their rejection of God. There is in the mystery of the cross a poignant meeting between the sweetness of God, manifested in the patience of Jesus, and the revolt of sinful man against God because this sweetness of God in the midst of the humiliations of the Son made obedient even unto death becomes intolerable to sinful man who finds his pride and violence exposed in it. The cry of Jesus on the cross is, in the last analysis, the supreme suffering of a love which sees itself rejected in the very gesture with which it opens itself out to the compassion and helpfulness of his brothers, whilst God appears as a silent witness or even an accomplice. The deepest suffering Jesus has to undergo is, on account of the unequalled quality of his filial love for the Father, to feel his heart shot through with feelings and thoughts of despair of God.

Is the cry from the cross then the expression pure and simple of this despair? No, for it is a cry of love and a prayer, where sinful man's greatest temptation—which is precisely to despair of God and in the effectiveness of his mercy—is taken up and turned back into measureless confidence. What proves this notion to us is the way in which John and Luke understood the death of Jesus as abandonment into the hands of the Father and as an ultimate testimony of obedience. Jesus had to open himself up to sinful man's spiritual drama in order to make of it the last word of his offering to the Father. In order to be able to give the Father everything that goes to make up the condition of sinful man, Jesus had not only to know and to go beyond the fear of death but also to know and to go beyond the fear of God, the fear of the Father, the fear that makes us picture the Father as disillusioning, deceitful and cruel. The suffering of Jesus consisted precisely in opening up his human sensibility to this fear of the Father whilst being quickened to the core of his being by the simplest possible and most complete love for the Father. It is on account of his love for the Father that Jesus experiences the spiritual suffering of contradiction and struggle in his relationship with the Father, and it was on account of his love for the Father that Jesus was able to let this final ordeal issue in the supreme abandonment of his life into the hands of the Father.

2. THE PROTEST OF THE SUFFERING JOB

What enables us to understand better the cry of Jesus on the cross is the comparison with the protest of Job. In so far as we can paint it in broad strokes, the protest of Job seems to be based on three complaints that he addressed to God. There is first of all the affirmation of his innocence, then the reproach that he is being tormented by God, and finally the protest at the inequality of men's destiny before God.

Job's affirmation of innocence is a cry of personal truth, whereas the accusations levelled at him by his friends are nothing but ritual charges (Job 22:5-9 and 20:19-23). Job is fully justified in priding himself on irreproachable conduct in the eyes of God and man. It is not just that he cared for the poor by giving them alms and hospitality but that he took pains to maintain the purity of his heart through the delicate way he regarded young girls (Job 31:1) and the constant and complete acceptance of the will of God (Job 1:20-22). It would, therefore, be wrong to think of Job's justice consisting merely in the material conformity to a rich landowner's code of propriety. He is conscious of a God who wants to find in his creatures an integrity of heart formed by filial obedience and adoration.

The second charge Job makes against God is that he torments him. It is not just that Job's ordeal breaks open the prevailing notion of a God who afflicts the wicked and protects and blesses the just, but that there is some indication of a reversal.

On this view, God is not content to test the just along with the wicked indifferently. No, it is as if God pits himself with particular ferocity against the innocent servant that Job is. God does not cease to watch Job whom he has picked as his target (Job 7:18-20). God becomes Job's accuser (Job 9:15), thereby paradoxically taking over from the adversary mentioned at the beginning of the sapiential story (Job 1:9 and 2:4-5). In the legal proceedings instituted against Job, God, the just judge, plays the role of the prosecutor and never stops spying on Job so as to catch him red-handed. The creator of all things, who has formed Job's flesh with his own hands, seems to take pleasure in crumbling him bit by bit in his own hands. The God of Job seems at times to be the complete opposite of the Creator and Father in some sort of deliberate perversion of his role towards man. God persists in surrounding Job with terrors and assaults him with acts of violence. In a word, God seems to have become the enemy of Job.

Job's third complaint is to do with the inequality of men's destiny in regard to divine justice. It is not just that God does not seem to pay attention to the integrity of men's conduct but that he seems to favour the unjust and the wicked since they succeed in everything, *pace* the too short-sighted wisdom of Job's friend. The wicked man seems for all the world to enjoy a special protection from God (Job 21:30). God remains deaf in the face of men's worst violence against the poorest in the community (Job 24:12).

The fact remains, however, that Job addresses his complaint to God himself in whom he persists in recognising the just judge. It is also a fact that Job, in however veiled a way, proclaims his hope in a God who will take his defence against God himself and who will give back his life and happiness in the eyes of all (Job 16:19-21 and 19:25-27), beyond death itself. The cry of Job is therefore a prayer addressed to God, a plea full of confidence. In any case the close of the book testifies to the innocence of Job, because God himself praises him for having spoken about him uprightly (Job 42:7-8). In this way God authenticates Job's speech of protest, albeit only after having shown him in a poetic manner, as in some sumptuous children's picture book, the unfathomable wonders of his creative providence. In short, God believes that Job was right in his point of view as long as he did not foreclose the mystery of wisdom that guides everything and that draws the universe and men's lives towards a new and unknown world, the world of God.

It would be a mistake to think that the Book of Job concludes flatly by coming back to where it began. The new gift that God gives Job is not limited to the magnificent reconstruction of his framework of life: it consists in the experience of his presence in the intimacy of listening to the revealing Word. Job finds himself enfolded more deeply in adoration and in the conviction of his littleness before the creator and master of all. Having disabused the wisdom of religious men of his time of its naïve presumptuousness, Job finds himself confronted directly by the wisdom of God. This goes far beyond any argued response to claims reaffirmed in the light of daily and verifiable experience. God does not even take the trouble to lift a corner of the secret of the future veiled by death. The response to Job consists in the affirmation of his constant and universal presence, in the gift of his presence: he is there everywhere and always, and so he has never left Job and could never abandon him. His presence may become invisible, but that is on account of the mystery of divine paternity: before his creator man can only remain a child very quickly bewildered when he loses his immediate bearings. The only light he has, in the end, is his certitude that God is always with him. This is the gift Job has received in his ordeal.

If we now return to the cry of Jesus on the cross, the two experiences evoked should illuminate each other: the figure of the just sufferer in the first alliance, and the passion of the holy one of God. The two experiences are connected in many external ways. Like Job, Jesus is abandoned by his friends to the insults and derision of his foes. Like Job, in fact much more so, he is attacked in his own flesh. Like Job, Jesus is surrounded by the shadow of death. But what makes Jesus most like Job, beyond these external similarities, is his innocence in the face of a God who seems to abandon him. At the same time, Jesus does not take up Job's complaints against a God perceived as his accuser, enemy, even executioner (Job 30:21).

All that Jesus brings out by his cry is the silence of God, which may be an attestation not exactly of his complicity with the violence of men or of his weakness, but at least of his permissiveness and the complete non-intervention in the justice of men. Jesus' God appears not as a Father who is transformed into a perverse destroyer of the work of his hands, but at least as a remote God who remains indifferent to the injustice of men, even when this touches his beloved Son who cries to him, imploring his help and deliverance.

Jesus' cry nevertheless goes far beyond Job's protest, because he poses a question about the nature and maintenance of the privileged relationship between the Father and his only Son. Job made his complaint to his creator, whereas Jesus' cry on the cross went up to his Father who is God. The depth of the spiritual drama in question is not in any way to be measured by the extent of the complaints but by the initial situation of intimacy with God which is then apparently put in doubt; Jesus' passion is not a repetition of Job's ordeal but the transposition to a much deeper plane. By this very token the suffering of Jesus brings to the question of Job a response that is above all of the order of witness rather than of explanation.

We could say that the cry of Jesus on the cross is not God's response to Job's question but a hearing on God's part in an extraordinary way of Job's question by making it be reformulated by his own Son come to take flesh of our flesh. In Jesus the Father raised the perfect man who shares his brothers' distress in every way and above all their spiritual distress, that is to say their fear of God the Father, their fear of being abandoned by him. Here again the letter to the Hebrews gives us teaching of an inexhaustible richness: 'In the days of his flesh, Jesus offered up prayers and supplications, with loud cries and tears, to him who was able to save him from death, and he was heard for his godly fear. Although he was a Son, he learned obedience through what he suffered; and being made perfect he became the source of eternal salvation to all who obey him, being designated by God a high priest after the order of Melchizedech' (Heb 5:7-10). Jesus who realised perfect obedience within himself, the loving return of the creature towards his creator, loving abandonment of the Son to his Father, nevertheless wanted out of solidarity with men his brothers, to taste the dregs of the most lacerating dereliction there can be, the anguish of being abandoned, not to say rejected by God.

And if Jesus was heard by the Father, it was not by obtaining from him the right to pass death by. He wanted to know death, the last ordeal of sinful man. If he was heard, it was through death, which was able to strike him down for an instant but not to keep him in its chains. As soon as Jesus accepted death, he recovered his glory as Son and was able to testify to the victory of divine love, stronger than death and all fear, in the presence of the just of the first alliance: '. . . being put to death in the flesh but made alive in the spirit, in which he went and preached to the spirits in prison' (1 Pet. 3:18-19). There is in the death of Jesus an unfathomable abyss of spiritual dereliction compared with the transient ordeal of Job, which was more superficial—in so far as it is possible to compare the reality with the figure. We do, however, also have to say that the resurrection of Jesus is completely different from a return to his previous condition. The resurrection of Jesus, of course, constitutes neither a revenge on his enemies nor a compensation for his total renunciation. The risen one keeps within himself his disposition of love and humility, patience and obedience. This does not prevent the glory of the risen Christ from wiping away all tears, all sadness, all doubt.

The witness that Jesus bears and that forms a living response to the questioning of Job is not, however, his welcome of the resurrection but his desire for the cross. If the cry of Jesus on the cross is made a little comprehensible by the act of complete abandonment in which it issues, it already finds a partial explanation in the desire that underlies it and that is the desire to offer up his life. The whole sense of the passion of Jesus derives from the fact that it is voluntary. Jesus wanted to undergo death in order to free us from sin. There was even in his resolute will that element of impatience that is the mark of love: 'I came to cast fire upon the earth; and would that it were already kindled! I have a baptism to be baptised with; and how I am constrained until it is accomplished!' (Luke 12:49-50). Jesus' desire is the deepest reality of his being human and of his redemptive suffering. This desire is at once the human expression and the human realisation of his divine being as Son completely turned towards the Father in adoration

E

and the offer of his life. It is because Jesus is wholly love of the Father in the passion of his desire that he suffered so much from carrying our fear of being abandoned by the Father on our behalf, a fear instigated by him who is the accuser of our sin.

3. THE SPIRITUALITY OF THE CROSS

The language of the cross reveals the wisdom of God in regard to all aspects of our Christian life but especially in regard to what happens to us in our ordeals and purifications. What gives the science of the cross its human truth and the authentic content of light and force for each of us is the love of God which the Holy Spirit instils into the heart of the baptised. The Holy Spirit, in wakening and ceaselessly developing in us the love for the Father guides us in the way of Jesus, the unique Son and first-born, which is a way of humility and obedience, of renunciation and total gift, the way of the cross. The more love of the Father there is in us, the more the gift becomes blessed and quickening, even in regard to the inescapable dispossession of and death to ourselves. When the love of God in us is not stronger than everything, the fear of death and the fear of God become contradictory obstacles on the way of the cross and we tend to fall back on the rather superficial device of projecting on to others the spiritual struggle which tears us apart.

The cry of Jesus on the cross is not a reproach against God, but the explosion of suffering in love. The communion between the Father and the incarnate Son finds its perfect human realisation only in the passion and the cross in which the Son draws all human life and his desire for life into his life for the Father. It is thus that the Son in his humanity is made perfect and accomplished in his obedience to the Father. In human terms the relationship between the Father and the Son is never so full as on the cross, when the Son gives back his life to the Father, led by the 'eternal Spirit' (Heb. 9:4). Love gives no explanation, but it makes a relationship with and against everything live. If it could be heard by our ears, the response of God to Jesus, as to Job, would simply be: '*I am* always with you.'

In this perspective, the cry of Jesus on the cross prolongs and deepens the protest of Job, for the absence and silence of the Father can disturb the Son much more that the withdrawal of the sovereign God of the universe, become a little enigmatic for a time in the eyes of his faithful servant. It is nevertheless in pressing Job's questioning to its limit that Jesus brings a response that is not an explanation but a presence of love. I should like to say that the love of Jesus for the Father allows him to put the strongest question there is because he is so sure of being heard and answered by the Father. The witness of Jesus is the complete simplicity of his filial love the depth of which is that of an ocean without bottom or bourn, the very love that is the divine life. Against this unfathomable ground of the mystery of the love of the Son for the Father, the cry from the cross is an appeal of love that draws its force from the quality of the relationship from which it springs. In sum, the sense of this cry goes beyond every attempt at interpretation, but in this very fact it invites us to enter into the relationship of the Son to the Father in adoration and the gift of our life not costing less than everything.

Translated by Iain McGonagle

Note

1. Paris, édition Brunscvicg, Section VII, fragment 553, p. 574. Pascal's meditation is centred on the agony and sorrow of Jesus, but we can find in this text a way of understanding the cry of Jesus on the cross.

PART IV

The Topicality of Job

Enrique Dussel

The People of El Salvador:
the Communal Sufferings of Job
(A theological reflection based on documentary evidence)

To Silvia Maribel Arriola,
a nun murdered in the parish of Zacamil in January 1981

We shall never forget what you did last year
When in San Roque we heard you speak
Vowing your life's service loud and clear
To the needs of the poor and the weak.

You shed your fresh and sparkling blood
For the hungry and downtrodden,
And now a thousand roses bloom
On your tender broken body.

E. D. Popular verses in memory of Silvia (Managua, 1983)

TO TRY to apply the message of the Book of Job, whether analogously or allegorically, to a whole people, can well appear a risky, if not an impossible undertaking. But remember the biblical figure or hermeneutical concept of the 'incorporating personality', used of the person of Israel, for example: a historical individual whose name is applied by analogy to the Hebrew *people*, to the 'remnant' of Israel, to Jesus, to the early Christian community (the 'new Israel'), to the Church itself as a whole. In this sense, Job can equally be *a* person or *a* people. There can be a collective Job, a Job-community. A suffering, persecuted, crucified Job-people.

I should make clear at the outset that I am writing of El Salvador in March 1983 and it is quite possible that in the near future the 'suffering people' will become the 'victorious people' and no longer be a suffering Job but a Moses setting out on the way through the desert, happy and full of hope, but no less responsible for its destiny; tempted, hungry, sometimes afflicted (like 'Nicaragua-in-the-desert' now—March 1983). Each people becomes different figures over the course of a few months or a few years when history

61

makes certain nations the agents of great social changes, as is happening today in Central America. Theology must learn to listen to events close to . . . or it will come too late . . . or too early. . . .

Next, I should say that I am using an interpretation of the Book of Job slightly different from the usual one.[1] It is agreed that it falls into three parts: Introduction—chs. 1-2; disputes with the 'comforters'—chs. 3-42:6; Epilogue—42:7-17. But I think I dissent from tradition by taking the second part (including the words of the 'cosmological' God: 38:1-41) as part of an act in which the God of Israel, the God of the poor, *absents himself*, ceases to show his face (*pnei* in Hebrew: Job 1:12 and 2:7), in order to allow Satan (*shatan* in Hebrew) to dominate the situation, the system, the overall drift of events. The comforters (Eliphaz, Bildad, Sophar and finally Elihu) would then be the *theologians of domination* who try to convince the suffering Job that he is guilty, that he is suffering because he has sinned, *thereby hiding the 'evil' that the system produces in the poor*. The system of domination, Satan and his 'associates', would have the dominated, the poor, feel guilty of their sufferings: all their arguments conspire to form a *theology of resignation*. Neither Job nor the people of El Salvador admit their arguments.[2]

1. LIKE JOB, THE PEOPLE OF EL SALVADOR KNOW THEIR SUFFERING[3]

Satan 'smote Job' (2:7), that is El Salvador, in recent times, first in 1932, when the army—already supported by North American businesses—murdered more than 30,000 peasants, including Sandina's comrade Farabundo Martí and the martyrs—among thousands—José Feliciano Ama and Chico Sánchez. This is only the affliction of recent times, because in fact the people of El Salvador has, since the particularly bloody Spanish conquest of the early sixteenth century, been continually oppressed, violated in all its rights.

But when Satan 'smote Job—El Salvador' for the second time in recent years, the violence was far more gruesome, and has till now accounted for the lives of 50,000 of the poor. Let us take two of them as examples:

Ana Coralia Martínez, 21. María Ercilia Martínez, 28. The district of Salinas. These two young women were dragged out their house at 2 a.m. by eight armed men (including Atilio Matute and J. Pacheco, both members of ORDEN, the others being members of the National Guard, all dressed in civilian clothes). They were next seen dead, with marks of cruel torture, raped, with bullet wounds. They were found on the banks of the El Angel canal, from where the National Guard of Apopa collected the bodies and took them to the morgue of the General Cemetery in the same town. These two girls were auxiliary Red Cross workers in Aguilares, and Ana Coralia was also Coordinator of Rutilio Grande's parish committee.[4]

Such documents are proof of the situation of the people in El Salvador, of their suffering, their martyrdom. All this has been going on for two decades, but the pace is now accelerating. The political organisation of the vanguard (the Popular Forces of Liberation—FPL, and the People's Revolutionary Army—ERP) began in the 1960s, and many Christians joined these forces from their beginnings. In fact, and this must always be borne in mind, these revolutionary forces would never have been popular, rooted in the history of the people, without the conscious and organic presence of the Christian participants. In 1980 the Coordinator of the Democratic Revolutionary Front (FDR) told me in Mexico that 'since the killings of '32, without the presence and organisation of Christians, with their peasant Base Communities, their Delegates of the

Word, the uprising would have been impossible. They were the first to organise the people'.

In the 1960s came the formation of Catholic Action and the organisation of a 'Christian democrat framework' with its 'Courses of social capacitation' (such as FUNPROCCOP, started by Mgr Chávez). This process was renewed with the coming of the Vatican Council. In 1967 CESPROP (the Centre for Social Studies and Popular Advancement) was founded, and in 1968 the bishops took part in the Medellín Conference. The experimentation with Base Communities went on growing, leading to the First National Pastoral Week, which was criticised by the bishops. This led the organiser of the Week, Fr Rutilio Grande (born in 1928, martyred in 1977) to declare: 'By criticizing the theology of liberation, the basis of the Pastoral Week, the Episcopal Conference has forgotten what Medellín said about it.'[5] A bulletin entitled *Justice and Peace: Study Notes* began to circulate among the country people, and did much to raise consciousness. In 1971 Fr Nicolas Rodríguez became the movement's first martyr.[6] This led the bishops to declare: 'In the face of the wave of violence and crime we appeal to the conscience of the Armed Forces and the Security Forces, and insist that they restrict their activities to the service which is their purpose and to no other.'[7] As the people grew in consciousness and organisation, so the repression grew, leading to the time of the second 'coming' of Satan, who has 'smitten' the people for the past seven years in the most appalling fashion:

Since 1974 such names as San Francisco Chinamequita, La Cayetana, Tres Calles, Santa Barbara, San Salvador Plaza Libertad, have acquired a tragic renown in the country. In all these places, in the name of prevention or repression, the lives of many of the people of El Salvador have been cut down by the State Security forces.[8]

The repression went on growing, culminating in the killing of 30 July 1975, when the security forces opened fire on a crowd of peaceful demonstrators. When Fr Mario Bernal was expelled, Rutilio Grande declared in a famous homily: 'I very much fear, my beloved brothers and sisters, that very soon the Bible, the Gospel, will no longer be able to cross our frontiers . . . because every page in it will be considered subversive.'[9]

On 22 February 1977 Mgr Oscar Arnulfo Romero was appointed Archbishop of San Salvador. On 27 February, Fr Alfonso Navarro celebrated a mass to deplore the electoral fraud, at which he said: 'If anything happens to me for telling the truth, you know who will be guilty.'[10] Three months later he was murdered. On 12 March Rutilio Grande was killed. His parish of Aguilares had been a training centre for hundreds of Community leaders—who were to be killed in their turn, one by one, over the coming years:

Aguilares is singing the precious song of liberation. We are the witnesses to this sorrow, to this separation. I feel it very close to my heart because as a Pastor I feel the sorrowing confidence of those who through the Church seek to meet those whom repression has scattered.

Mgr Romero, *Homily at the Funeral Mass for Rutilio Grande.*[11]

And the scale of killing went on increasing: till now 50,000 poor, country people are dead: a real historical and community Job. On 29 September 1978 Mgr Romero declared: 'The Catholic Church of El Salvador is being forced back to the time of the catacombs.' On 26 November Fr Ernesto Barrera was murdered. Then came Puebla, from which Mgr Romero sought support in a letter, trying at least to postpone his death—which he clearly saw would come at any moment. On 24 March 1980 he was martyred.

I should like to pay special tribute to Sr Silvia Maribel Arriola, who as a nun joined the Farabundo Martí National Liberation Front (FMLN). She was working with the army medical team on the Western 'Feliciano Ama' Front, in the Zacamil district of the Department of Santa Ana in January 1981 when their camp was bombed by the army. She is a heroine of Latin American liberation, a nun, a woman, a consecrated person, a guerrilla fighter, part of the sufferings of the historical Job of Latin America:

We are victims of the most cruel tortures, beaten and maltreated in every imaginable way: we have electric shocks applied to the tenderest parts of our bodies—genitals, soles of our feet, head, tongue, eyes, ears. . . . We are suffocated by the 'hood'. . . . We have acids applied to our tissues, which eat away our flesh and cause terrible pain. We are hung in the air in various ways for long periods of time while being hit and beaten on different parts of the body. And we women, besides undergoing these tortures, are sexually humiliated in every possible way, having to put up with the worst violations by our captors who prey on our defenceless bodies like possessed beasts.[12]

Written by one of the 'disappeared' in a prison run by the Army supported by the United States.

And the same document goes on: 'Jesus Christ was cowardly tortured and put to death for the sole crime of proclaiming the Good News of the Kingdom of God to the poor'; and: 'Only faith and a deep conviction that the oppressed will triumph enable us to stand up to the trials with which we are faced.' Community Job, suffering Job, Job in history!

2. LIKE JOB, THE PEOPLE OF EL SALVADOR KNOW THEY ARE INNOCENT[13]

The suffering people know they are innocent; at least they know they are not suffering because of any sin they may have committed, consciously or unconsciously. '. . . who prey on our defenceless bodies like possessed beasts. So do the oppressors discharge their fury, so do they pretend that we should *pay for crimes that we have never committed.*'[14] One has to realise that the crimes of which they are accused, the sin of Job's 'comforters', is simply not conforming to the system that oppresses them. The mere fact of saying 'I am hungry!' is sufficient reason to be accused of sin, of subversion, of being guerrillas, communists or whatever. When Ronald Reagan justifies the sending of 110 million dollars to help the army in El Salvador before the US Congress, he explains to a journalist who asks him: 'How bad is the military situation?': 'It is not good, but Salvadoran soldiers have proved that when they are well trained, led and supplied, they can *protect* the people from guerrilla *attacks*.'[15] And referring to the military of Central America, the President of the most powerful nation in the world today said: 'We worshipped the same God. . . .'[16]

One can now understand what Michael Novak, Catholic theologian at the 'Institute for Democracy and Religion' (IDR) and the 'American Enterprise Institute' meant when he said about El Salvador: 'Events in Iran and Nicaragua have begun to show public policy analysts that they omit religion—specifically, the ideas of theologians—from their calculations at their peril.'[17] That is, the present-day capitalist system of the 'centre' justifies its actions in the name of God (Reagan and the Central American military 'worship the same *God*'). The question of religion then becomes essential, as Novak says, because it is the level on which the acts of violence perpetrated by the military in order to save capitalism in El Salvador are ultimately justified. The 'aid' in arms used to kill the people, to 'smite' Job—are justified on the grounds that the miltary are defending the people from the guerillas (when the facts are the opposite, that the people with the help of the guerrillas are defending themselves from the attacks of the military supported by the United States). So the 'comforters', the *theologians of domination* (formerly theologians of resignation who convinced the people of their sin and exhorted them to patience and hope of a happy life *after death*, whereas now they justify theologically the very use of repressive violence: an explicit theology of domination) have the task of 'convincing', of creating a 'consensus' in favour of the violent means to be adopted in order to paralyse the people through terror. This terror—which does not stop at the most horrible tortures but even beheads the bodies of those it has murdered or 'explodes' them with bombs placed in their guts so as to frighten off the others, leaving the bodies in lanes, on city and town streets, or even in their own houses—which has adopted political forms, seeks to 'immobilise' the people—Job. But the people do not accept any supposed blame. They know who the guilty ones are: Satan:

Formerly the Church used to put about the idea that the world was evil because we were evil: brutal, womanisers, idiots, and the solution was always in confession and repentance. Now we here are beginning to understand that God's plan was for us to be masters of the world and of our history and, as the prophet Hosea said, for that which is not-yet-a-people to become a people and the people of God. If this is to happen, the Christian community has to be the witness and leaven of the new people. Gone is the time for letting ourselves be deceived by Parties that have nothing to do with us.[18]

Thus one document. And another:

Here in El Salvador there are hundreds of political prisoners who are being held for having done no more than be faithful to the example of Jesus Christ. We are deprived of our liberty because we follow the teachings of our Martyr Archbishop Mgr Romero, who once said: 'If we Christians feel ourselves to be followers of Jesus we will understand that solidarity with the people to the end is a matter of being true to our faith.'[19]

There is never a hint of a consciousness of any sin of the people behind the persecution, torture and suffering. Never. The sinners are the military, the ruling classes, the United States; they are the active subject of sin. The suffering of the people is an objective effect of sin. The innocent suffer the consequences of the practice of domination. Faith alone 'keeps alive the flame of hope', another document says, 'and feeds it so that our spirit can stand this martyrdom'.[20] The suffering people, Job, is convinced of the essence of revelation: 'God never does wrong (*yarshyah*), do not doubt that!' (Job 34:12). 'Wrong' is the product of domination, and the dominated who suffer its effects know they are innocent; they know that the dominators make them suffer (and it is in this 'making suffer' that sin consists), and that the dominator is Satan. The people of El Salvador know this final truth; Job did not, though the author of the Book of Job did, and this is the only reason why he wrote the book.

The death of martyrs—such as Rutilio Grande or Oscar Romero—shows up (like the practice of the Cross of Christ) the evil of the system: it reveals the sin of the system. But the only way for this sin to be seen *as sin* is for the just who suffer to declare themselves innocent of their own sufferings. The theology that shows the suffering of the just as the effective object of the sin of injustice committed by the sinner because he dominates, is a theology of liberation. The theology that justifies the use of violence—even in the name of 'God' (in reality the Fetish, the Idol) or of Western Christian civilisation (or in the name of its 'enduring' values) or tries to convince the suffering people that they have sinned, is a theology of domination. This is why the theology of liberation is proving so unpopular *politically* (even though it is intrinsically *religious*) in El Salvador. It de-legitimises oppression and the sufferings of Job and deprives *Satan's collaborators* of their 'good conscience'.

3. BEYOND JOB: FUTURE MEMORIES

But the people of El Salvador, going beyond Job, have before their eyes (remembering these events they immerse themselves in the future of the whole country liberated in a short while when victory is won) the reality of the project that is *now being brought about*. It is as though in the midst of his sufferings Job could at one and the same time enjoy the happiness of having his riches and his family restored to him, and his health. Let a nun, Sister Rosa, be the last witness:

'Since the sixties, the Church in El Salvador has discovered a deep dynamism. . . . There has been a rich experience of conversion of religious communities under the inspiration of Mgr Chávez. They have gone out into the desert to learn from the people, away from their Catholic schools. . . . Several have been expelled, three North American sisters have been murdered, after being raped. Sr Silvia Arriola was murdered; I think she must be the first warrior nun of the Latin American martyrology, like Joan of Arc. . . .'

'Sister' asked a journalist, 'what responsibilities do you have here, in a liberated zone of the Front?'

'Well, I teach, and I try to organise seven centres plus the same number of camps which belong to the zone in which we are operating.'

'Do you call yourself a fighting nun?'

'In the sense that all of us are at war and have a place in the fighting forces, yes. Any struggle against injustice is war. The very act of teaching people who are denied this right to knowledge is a struggle against unjust illiteracy.'

'Why did you abandon your habit to join the guerillas?'

'First let me say that I have in no way abandoned my habit. I consider myself fully acting as a nun, more so than ever before in my life.'

'Did you tell your superior what you proposed to do? What did she say?'

'She knew that I had been working for a long time to help the poor, particularly the country poor. She knows that there are Christian people in these hills and understands my need in conscience to be with them. She went through all this with me and has no objection to my continuing here now that the people have even more need of me. I have not fled from anything; I am just going on with my people.'

'But education here also means political education.'

'Or rather political education has implications on other levels. The children now know what the United States are and what they mean for us. They know they are an imperialist power and we are part of their strategic plan. They know what an oligarchy is, who the military Junta are. . . .'

'Could this struggle to free the people be called a Christian conflict?'

'The Church has played its part in awakening social consciousness, helping the masses to discover their rights, which led to struggles to claim their rights starting in their own communities, until they discovered that there were organisations of peasants, of workers, of farmers, and realised that love for one's neighbour meant being organised and so came to swell the ranks of the revolution. Mgr Romero once said: "sometimes, not being organised can be a sin." And when this is happening the only thing we can do is be with the people, giving them the pastoral care of sharing our lives with them. You must know that there are parts where 99 per cent of the population are organised Christians, thirsting for justice, peace and unity.'[21]

This is more than Job could see!

Translated by Paul Burns

Notes

1. See N. H. Tur-Sinai *The Book of Job. A new Commentary* (Jerusalem 1957) (a fine work by a believing Jew); *Job: a new Translation* by M. H. Pope (New York 1982) with bibliography; H. H. Rowley *The Book of Job* (Grand Rapids 1980) with bibliography; F. Andersen *Job: an Introduction and Commentary* (London 1976); Driver-Gray *A Critical and Exegetical Commentary on the Book of Job* (Greenwood 1977); *The Book of Job* ed. C. Habel (Cambridge 1975), to give a brief bibliography of what is available in English. On the interpretation of Satan, see Kittel *TWNT*, VII, 151-165 II, 69ff. and I, 194ff.

2. For this interpretation, bear in mind that, at first, Job was happy (1:1-6). Then Satan appears (1:6) and sets out to tempt Job ('And Satan left the Lord's presence'—1:12). But as Job does not fall, he tests him a second time, with the same expression being used in 2:7. And from this moment till Yahweh's final intervention (2:7b-42:7, since the intervention of the 'cosmological God' in 38:1-41:26 is ambiguous) *Job is in Satan's hands*, that is in the hands of the system of oppression, the system based on the Fetish, on the Idol, even on a 'cosmological God' who is *not historical* and does not speak of the poor and the oppressed (an ambiguous God can also be a justification for a system of oppression). Once Yahweh leaves the scene, Satan enters the action: 'and he smote Job . . .' (2:7b). Now it is Satan who is responsible for his suffering, not any pretended sin on Job's part, nor any act on Yahweh's part, since he did not smite him nor order it to be done, but merely permitted it: 'All that he has is in your hands' (1:12) and 'He is in your hands . . .' (2:6). The God of the poor has nothing to do with what happens next, which is the responsibility of the Devil. *Job knows this*, and this is what the writer of the book is showing: God does not cause the sufferings of the poor; Satan does—the 'system', the dominator, 'Sin', Evil.

3. Thanks to many friends in El Salvador, I have many *direct accounts*, such as letters written from prison, proving what is happening to this martyred people.

4. This is one example among thousands. This is one witness from seventy-seven in the three pages dealing with the region of Aguilares alone, where Fr Rutilio Grande, SJ, was parish priest and martyr. In January and February 1980 alone there were seventy-seven murders in the holy Jesuit's parish. I have sent *Concilium* a photocopy of these three pages, along with other unpublished documents from which I quote, as evidence of the accuracy of what I am telling.

5. Anon. *Rutilio Grande* (Salvador 1978). For this history see R. Cardenal 'Historia de la Iglesia en El Salvador' in *Hist. gen, de la Iglesia en América Latina*, VI (Salamanca 1983); also E. Dussel *De Medellín a Puebla* (Mexico 1979) pp. 231ff.; R. Sol *Para entender El Salvador* (San José 1980); *El Salvador: un pueblo perseguido, testimonio de cristianos* (Lima 1981); P. Richard and G. Meléndez *La Iglesia de los pobres en América Latina* (San José 1980).

6. ICI 400 (1972) p. 19.

7. *Praxis de los Padres de América Latina* (Bogota 1979) p. 323.

8. *Persecución de la Iglesia en El Salvador* (El Salvador 1977) p. 12. See also 'Muerte y persecución de campesinos' in *SPES* (Lima) 31/2 (1977) pp. 34-40; 'Padecerán persecución por mi causa' in *MIEC-JFCI* 16-18 (Lima 1978) pp. 174ff. For all his seventy-three years, Archbishop Luis Chávez y González is still growing: 'In this country, coffee—in the hands of the oligarchy and the North Americans—is eating men. As Salvadoreans and Christians, as priests and bishops we are dismayed . . . by the material and spiritual violence our country is suffering' (ICI 472, 1975, p. 30).

9. *Signos de lucha y esperanza* (Lima 1979) pp. 256-261. He goes on: 'I very much fear that if Jesus Christ were to come again as he did then, down from Chalatenago to Salvador, he would not get further than Apopa with his preaching and accusations. They would seize him in the hills of Guazapa, and take him before a whole lot of Supreme Courts as unconstitutional and subversive. Without a doubt, my brothers, they would crucify him again. . . . They are without reason and with their lack of reason want to break the mould of truth, which cannot be broken with a finger or with brute force.' This brute force was soon to cause his martyrdom.

10. 'Padecerán . . .' the article cited in note 8, at p. 182. See *Excelsior* (Mexico) 27 March 1977, p. 3.

11. *ECA* (San Salvador) 344 (1977) p. 433.

12. Document in my possession from COPPES (Committee for Political Prisoners in El Salvador) June 1982. This is how the four North American nuns, two of them from Maryknoll, were martyred.

13. The speeches of the 'comforters' always include an accusation that Job has sinned and is suffering on account of this: 4:7; 8:6; 11:11; 15:35; 18:5; 20:29; 22:5; 25:4; (27:1?); 34:32. Job always replies with an assertion of his innocence, in speech after speech: 7:20; 9:20; 13:23; 16:17; 19:5; 21:7ff.; 23:10; 27:5; 31:16-40. The 'cosmological God'—who can equally be an Idol—puts the main question: 'Dare you . . . put me in the wrong that you may be right?' (40:8). In effect, if the sufferer *is not* a sinner then the one who makes him suffer is not God *but Satan*. Not accepting guilt is prophetic criticism of the evil of the system: 'The truth is, God does no wrong' (34:12), so the one who does wrong is Satan, and *his angels, sinners*.

14. Document quoted in note 12 above.

15. *The New York Times* 10 March 1983, p. 6, col. 2.

16. *Ibid.* col. 6.

17. *Toward a Theology of the Corporation* (Washington 1981), Preface. This sets out to examine the following thesis: 'Some theologians today write as if corporations were *evil* (*sic*) forces and, indeed, as if democratic capitalism as a whole were incompatible with Christianity' (p. 5). Novak goes so far as to quote Isaiah 53:2-3 (the Suffering Servant), commenting: 'I would like to apply these words to the modern business corporation, a much despised incarnation of God's presence in this world' (p. 33).

18. Document in my possession (copy with *Concilium*).

19. *Ibid.*

20. *Ibid.*

21. *Ibid.*

Jean Collet

From Job to Bergman:
Anguish and Challenge

'THINK OF Gethsemane, Pastor. All the disciples had fallen asleep. They had understood nothing (. . .). And He remained alone. It must have caused him very great suffering. Understanding that no one had understood anything. . . . But that still wasn't the worst! When Christ had been nailed to the cross and was hanging there, amid all his suffering, he cried out: "My God, my God, why hast thou forsaken me?" (. . .) Christ was seized by great doubt during those last moments before he died. That *must* have been the most frightful of his sufferings? I mean the silence of God. Isn't that true, Pastor?' The man who speaks these words is the beadle in Bergman's film *The Communicants* (*Winter Light*). He is a cripple, enduring terrible physical suffering. He reads the story of the Passion to while away the hours of insomnia, and relates his thoughts to the pastor: the death agony of Christ, the pain, are nothing in comparison with the *anguish*. Finding that you are misunderstood, excluded, abandoned, is an experience which hurts more than any physical suffering. To feel rejected, not only by men but by God himself, confronted by the silence of God 'at the very time when you need someone you can rely on', is to reach an extreme point, an anguish which is absolute (*ab.solu*: loosened, unbound) as if your heart were being torn apart, your body dismembered, pulled limb from limb. The crucifixion, with its attendant tortures—the limbs broken and racked, the heart pierced—would then be merely the outward sign of absolute anguish, the bursting apart of the self, left alone with its own truth, blasted, burned, decomposed. 'I have become like dust and ashes.' It is Job who is speaking (30:19). '. . . amid the crash they roll on' (30:14). 'Such you have now become to me; you see my calamity, and are afraid' (6:21).

The Communicants (1962) is the central film of Bergman's famous trilogy (with *Through a Glass Darkly*, 1961, and *The Silence*, 1963). Bergman was forty-two years old when he decided to devote three films to what he calls 'a regression': from certainty to the silence of God, from Faith to the absence of God. The regression was a definitive one. In a later interview, Bergman concluded: 'the problem (of God) is no longer with me',[1] 'I have therefore stopped blaming God and the World'.[2] Far from deploring this regression, I would, myself, see in it the unmistakable sign of an inspiration which is sincere, scrupulous and profound. It is because God is absent, because he does not answer, because there is this intolerable 'face to face' encounter with anguish, that the film-director can and must create. This paradox is only an apparent one. It is this very

69

same paradox which makes it so hard to read the Book of Job. Job, too, confronts absolute anguish, calls upon a God who does not answer: 'If one wished to contend with him, one could not answer him once in a thousand times' (9:3). 'Behold, I cry out, "Violence!" but I am not answered; I call aloud, but there is no justice' (19:7). 'I cry to thee and thou dost not answer me' (30:20). An echo of this experience comes, in *Wild Strawberries* (1957), in the poem recalled by old Doctor Isak Borg: 'Where is the friend whom everywhere I seek? As day breaks, my desire is but increased. As day flies, still I find him not, though my heart burns within me. I see his traces everywhere. . . .'

Why should the absence of God provide the foundation for the creation of a work of art? Quite simply because man must lose all his certainties, all that constitutes his being, enables him to stand firm, defines him, encloses him, if he is to start out on the path of creation and fruitfulness. Bergman's nobility does not lie in making films in order to *say* something, to make some sort of affirmation, to deliver a 'message'; it lies, on the contrary, in delivering himself of his anguish, projecting onto the screen the ridiculous, pitiable puppets which, in truth, we are. Thus he becomes reunited with that defenceless child, the secret source of all creative impulses. Because he is afraid, because he is alone, because he knows that he must leave his father and mother. The work is born—like all living creatures—out of a painful separation. It tears us apart. Abandoning and being abandoned is the necessary condition of birth and creation. This is a truth which the modern world cannot bear, this increasingly foetal world in which everything—politics, institutions, speeches—combines to keep men in a permanent state of dependence, whimpering, stunted creatures, clustered together in the 'body of society', that monstrous womb which never gives birth, that sterile, constipated belly, constantly devouring and never being delivered of a child. Anguish is what wrings the heart and stomach of Job: 'My heart is in turmoil, and is never still' (30:27).

Bergman goes back to the same sensations to portray the birth of amorous desire in *Smiles of a Summer Night* (1950): 'It starts in your chest. And then it grips hold of your stomach and your knees turn to jelly. . . .' Doubtless, it is in his most tragic, 'despairing' films that Bergman allows this distress to burst forth; as we shall see, it corresponds precisely to the ordeal of Job. Agnes, the heroine of *Cries and Whispers* (1972), is suffering from cancer (probably of the womb). Unlike her two sisters, she has never known a man, never married. She is going to die in the house where she was born, the family home in the country, the 'mother-house'. In her diary she writes: 'Sometimes I want to put my hands over my face and never take them away again'.[3] Job: '. . . on my eyelids is deep darkness' (16:16). 'My eye has grown dim from grief' (17:7). Agnes: 'What is to become of me, me and my loneliness?' Job: '. . . my eye will never again see good. The eye of him who sees me will behold me no more' (7:7-8). Agnes: 'Long days, silent evenings, and the nights without sleep. What shall I do with all this time which is surging over me?' Job: 'When I lie down I say, "When shall I arise?" But the night is long, and I am full of tossing till the dawn' (7:4). Perhaps Bergman was inspired to create the heroine of *Cries and Whispers* by reading the Book of Job? That is not important. What must be noted here is, for Job and Agnes, a suffering which is worse than death. Both see themselves as *reduced to nothing*: by the disease which gnaws at them; even more, by the friends, the sisters, who drive them out and condemn them, who no longer wish to see them. Some time after her death, Agnes reappears to her sisters: 'I cannot leave you. . . . Can no one help me? . . . Stay with me until I'm no longer afraid. It's all so empty around me. . . . You must come nearer. . . .' Her sisters, terrified, run away. Only the servant, Anna, sits down on the deathbed, takes Agnes on her lap and stays with her, in the attitude of a Pietà. A fleeting but unforgettable image of a strange maternity, as if Anna's tenderness helped Agnes to die—to pass over, beyond anguish—to be born out of anguish. In other words, to allow herself to become (come *to be*) merely that absence to which others (God) consign her. Then, there is a genuine *dénouement* (unravelling, unbinding). The film ends, after Agnes's death, in a strange serenity. Anna reads Agnes's diary. The film evokes, through the words and the pictures, the harmony between the three sisters. Agnes is dead, but there remain her words, Anna's voice and Bergman's film. There remain the spirit of the cinema and the soul of Agnes, that mysterious breath which gives life to every work born of anguish. The voice murmurs: 'The people I love most in the world were near me. I could hear them talking quietly.' Words which both ratify and deny their separation. A final stratagem by which a *presence* is affirmed because it no longer exists: 'I could feel the nearness of their bodies, the warmth of their hands. . . .' To express this harmony one needs the story which has just been told, the illusion of the cinematic image, the magic of the actors on a screen, and that final confidence in which Bergman the director seems at one with Agnes: 'I wanted those moments to last forever'.

The Book of Job is neither an apologia for resignation nor an outburst of rebellion. It is the story of human anguish, the necessary condition of being born into the Spirit. In the horrible, dizzying void which suffering creates within and around us, the voice of Job, and of Bergman's characters, issues a defiant challenge. God is silent. There is no answer. God is indistinguishable from the Omnipotence of Evil. We are surely reminded here of the knight in *The Seventh Seal* (1956), playing chess with Death. He is seeking God; he discovers only death, violence and anguish. Among so many disappointing encounters I recall the one with the little witch, a child condemned to torture and the stake 'because she has had dealings with the Devil'. The knight approaches her; he too wishes to meet the Devil, 'ask him about God. Surely *he* must know. . . .' The child: 'Look into my eyes. Can you see him?' 'I can see the fear set deep in your eyes, an empty fear. That is all.'

Bergman's films, before and after the Trilogy, seek to explore that emptiness. And the omnipresence of Evil. Sometimes, even, it is the representatives of the Christian God who unleash Evil. Take, for example, the Lutheran bishop, Vergerus, in *Fanny and Alexander* (1982). He knows nothing but the Law, which enables one to separate truth from falsehood, good from evil. Because he is on the side of the Law, of order, he plays, on his own, the part of the three 'friends' of Job, those very men who condemn him. They speak with the voice of authority, of all authorities. Their words *indicate* Evil, whereas Job *indicts* it. To indicate Evil is to circumscribe it, to close up the abscess. Job's defiant challenge provokes, confronts, opens up the wound, lets the Evil flow out and the horror pour forth, right to the end. In *Cries and Whispers* there is an astonishing passage in Agnes's diary, which Bergman finally left out: 'Then, I take refuge in my despair and allow it to consume me. I have noticed that if I try to avoid it or to keep it in the background, everything gets more difficult. It is better to open yourself up, to welcome what torments or hurts you, not to close your eyes to it or hide from it as I used to do before.'[4] Bergman's films, like the Book of Job, are a *challenge* which, because it lays itself open to Evil—instead of repressing it—reveals the truth of a terrible Game in which man's greatness, his spirit, his soul, his divinity, is to fulfil himself in the silence and the absence and the anguish of God. 'Yes, why not try to picture the anguish of God?' asks Philippe Némo, at the end of his fine book *Job et l'excès du mal*.[5] It is by showing the anguish of Jesus, at the end of *The Communicants*, that Bergman destroys the image of the God who reassures: the God who corresponds to our desire, the mirror-image of our petition. Speaking of *The Communicants* with the director Vilgot Sjöman, Bergman remarked: 'In this film I settle my accounts with Daddy-God, the God of autosuggestion, the God who inspires confidence.'[6] I should like to emphasise the paradoxical ending of this film which anticipates, twenty years before, the theatrical dénouement of *Fanny and Alexander*. Having listened to the sacristan recalling the distress of Jesus ('My God, why, why hast thou forsaken me?'), the pastor decides to conduct worship in an almost empty church. 'With his pale face full of anguish, he proclaims: "Holy, Holy, Holy is the Lord God Almighty. The whole earth is full of his glory . . ." '.[7] There is the anguish, and, nevertheless, 'the ritual' (this was to be the title of another of Bergman's films). The game. The liturgy as the setting for the challenge to God. The representation of that challenge, defying everything and everybody. Even in an empty church. If God, and the *faithful* are absent, there remain the celebration, the theatre, the eternal debate in which the Other hides so that we shall seek him. 'Our soul likes to think that the soul of God, seeking ours, goes through hell, as ours does, during that anxious waiting. Anxious, because it does not know whether our soul will surrender itself.'[8]

Here, the experience of Bergman, the ordeal of his pastor link up with the thoughts of Bernanos's country priest: 'I believe more and more that what we call sadness, anguish, despair, as if to persuade ourselves that these are particular moods of the soul, is the soul itself. I believe that, since the Fall, man's condition is such that he càn no longer perceive anything, within or outside himself, except in the form of anguish.'[9] A fortunate anguish which enables us to come to birth—to act, to speak. To be born into the spirit, the theatre, the cinema and every form of creation. It is this anguish, running through Bergman's latest film, which bears *Fanny and Alexander* 'towards the joy' of the final celebration (the representation of a twofold birth). The Law kills. In *Fanny and Alexander*, the bishop is morbid, sterile and destructive. He destroys himself. Alone, perhaps, the challenge is fruitful. That of Bergman. That of Job. Fundamentally, Job is a great artist.

Translated by L. H. Ginn

Notes

1. S. Björkman, T. Manns, J. Sima *Le Cinéma selon Bergman* (Paris 1973) p. 238.

2. *Ibid.* p. 350.

3. Ingmar Bergman's introductory notes to the scenario of *Cries and Whispers*, *L'Avant-scène cinéma*, no. 142 (décembre 1973) p. 15.

4. *Ibid.*

5. Philippe Némo *Job et l'excès du mal* (Paris 1978).

6. 'Journal des *Communiants' Cahiers du cinéma* no. 165 (jeudi 20 juillet 1961).

7. Ingmar Bergman *Une Trilogie* (Paris 1964) p. 196.

8. Philippe Némo *op. cit.* p. 233.

9. Georges Bernanos *Journal d'un curé de campagne* (Bibliothèque de la Pléiade) p. 1183.

Marc Bochet

Job in Literature

Hé, très Doux Dieu, aide-moi
En ce besoin, en cet émoi. . . .
                    (*Mystère de la patience de Job,* fifteenth century)

THE SUFFERING of the innocent upright man is a rich and age-old theme in
literature. It can be traced down the centuries, from the Assyrio-Babylonian
inscriptions—'What evil have I done?'—right through to Claudel, in countless
anguished works that tell the harsh caprice of gods or Fate at some broken man's
expense.

In the Judaised West, this long literary meditation may well have its origin in the
Book of Job. Job appears in it closely connected with our weariness of life and as an
essential figure of our human wretchedness; a representative figure poised between
aggressiveness and inertia, acceptance and revolt. He is frequently referred to when
suffering writers assert that their suffering is not a result of just punishment, but can only
have been caused by some absurd twist of fate. The purpose of this article is to outline a
'Joban' area in imaginative French literature.

To enrich their repertory, medieval religious dramatists would draw freely on Old
Testament texts, and the Book of Job especially, 'because of the terrible trials he
suffered with resignation.'[1] The most successful of the verse adaptations of Job's story is
the fifteenth-century fifty-seven character *Mystère de la patience de Job*. The character
of Job, it should be noted, is dramatic by nature. He moves from the silence of despair to
the silence of adoration; his cries of suffering spiral up, his gesticulations are those of the
racked. His tragedy is the tragedy of the *actor* as defined by Artaud, or more
recently by Tadeusz Kantor in *Le Théatre de la mort*: 'Now, out of the general circle of
religious custom and rite (. . .), there has stepped *someone* who had just rashly
decided to detach himself from the cultural community.'[2] Job's frenzy is the liberation of
a *fury*. In essence, this fury is dramatic, but it is found in poetry and the novel as well as
drama.

The dereliction of Villon with no recourse but God is the dereliction of Job at the
height of his wretchedness: 'My days have fled away as, says Job, do the threads of a
piece of cloth . . .' (*Testament* 11. 217-219). Du Bellay also, the 'puniest' of creatures,
makes an act of adoration: 'Though I be but vile decay, yet such as I am, I am thy
creature' (*Hymne chrétien*). For Rabelais, Job is a rich and (mis-)married man, but in
general he was seen by sixteenth-century writers as a stoic, an example of constancy in

trials beyond our control: in Chassignet's *Job ou la fermeté*, for example, he was to some extent desacralised, and turned into an ethical model. After that, with the *précieux* salons, he became an increasingly secular figure, until in the celebrated seventeenth-century quarrel between the Uranists and the Jobelins about the sonnets of Voiture and Benserade, he replaced the great damned figures of mythology in the thematics of love. Instead of 'My suffering is greater than Ixion's' to express the peak of suffering, it became a source of entertainment to say 'My suffering is greater than Job's':

> Though he suffered incredible ill,
> He lamented and vented his woes;
> But my own are more wretched still.

These society games could easily have transformed Job into a mere figure of rhetoric. But he rapidly reappeared as a tragic figure in the words of Fr Surin, Pascal, Racine and Bossuet. Racine's Hippolyte, a virtuous young man damned by the gods, has been compared with him; La Fontaine's woodcutter may be partly based on him, as may the Pauper in Molière's *Dom Juan*.

In the eighteenth century, mainly with Voltaire, Job became the *escarmentado*,[3] the man who has been driven out, cast out. When Frederick II read *Candide*, he exclaimed: 'It's Job in modern dress',[4] and the story is indeed constructed on the same pattern as the biblical book, with the hero being wealthy initially, being driven out from his happy state, undergoing a series of trials, knowing the temptation of despair and revolt, and returning to the starting point to recover, as it were, his original joy. Just as Job's idol, a reassuring and protective God, must perish, and the hero awaken in the seemingly most absurd suffering to the terrible reality of a faceless God with impenetrable ways, so Candide must leave behind him the too facile philosophy of Pangloss, and learn from the harshness of existence a more courageous art of living. Voltaire's other stories tell similar tales of blistering catharsis.

The Job of Enlightenment philosophy is a Job who, in the bitter lessons of experience, finds reasons for hope and action. But the Job of Romanticism will be a model of man's sadness, his restlessness, his longing for the infinite. He will be referred to more and more frequently: by Chateaubriand, who with his sister translated 'the saddest passages of Job'; by Lamartine, whose sorrowful soul was in harmony with that of Job; by Victor Hugo who saw him as one of the beacons of mankind, 'a Titan of the dunghill'; and by Vigny, whose *Moïse* has recently been compared to the Book of Job. Job was now multi-faceted indeed, but with a special fascination for the poets, who saw his story as a tragedy of incomprehension and persecution like their own: 'Let me sleep the sleep of the earth.' As the century went by, emphasis on the suffering of an upright man gave way to a more philosophic stress. After Renan's translation, Job came to be seen as, for example, a saviour of humanity in Pierre Leroux's five-act drama, or by contrast, with Léon de Rosny, as a sceptic unable to solve the riddle of destiny.

But at the end of the century, the modern dimension of Job, with man abandoned in an absurd world, and condemned to the unrelenting misery of a sordid, larval existence, came to the fore. Flaubert was to make him one of his bedside books. With Rimbaud and Lautréamont began a stream of bitter sarcasms against a cruel and jealous God: 'I saw the Creator kindling his pointless cruelty, feeding the fires in which old men and children were dying.'[5]

In Verlaine and Apollinaire, dereliction changed from protest to invocation of the God of solace: 'Oh God who knows my pain, you who gave me it, what will become of me . . .' (*Alcools*).

At the start of the twentieth century, Job had become a figure Kierkegaardian in his anguish; he spoke, whether in resignation or revolt, not 'with magisterial detachment, but as a living example, out of his own experience'.[6] He was freedom painfully gestating a Reply that did not come, and it was this that brought him so close to us and impressed so many twentieth century writers. In *Si le grain ne meurt*, Gide confessed that the Book of Job had a decisive influence on him in his childhood: 'There is no doubt that this book made a most vivid impression on me.' Claudel wrote an impassioned commentary on it, and saw Job as the image of the poet 'whose language is inadequate to express the reality he perceives'.[7] For Bernanos, Job's dunghill was the world in its opaqueness, man in his anguished struggle in the darkness, the writer himself straining exhausted to bring his work to birth: 'I shall send you Job's dunghill today without fail';[8] the Abbé Donissan and Chantal tell the story of Job whose cry was wrung 'from his hard Jewish heart by universal malice'.[9] For Malraux, the agnostic thirsting for transcendence, Job was the first to dare to challenge God in his silence, when he posited him as the Wholly Other.[10] Camus omitted him from his history of revolt, doubtless because he saw him as an image of repentant man 'covered in ashes', like Clamence in *La Chute* or as, in *La Peste*, he is presented by Father Paneloux or represented by Dr Rieux, full of courage in a disintegrating world.[11] In Julien Green, for whom union with God requires the breaking of man, there is constant reference to Job: 'Whenever the chase round Paris left me weary, I would sit on a bench and read Job.'[12] Simone Weil, who in *Attente de Dieu* is wholly absorbed in Job's cry, shows that the main cause of his suffering is not knowing if he is right or wrong, and that he can no longer understand the testimony of his own conscience, so great is his despair.

But today more than ever before, in the convulsions of the post-war years, we who have witnessed the atomic bomb and the concentration camps, who are witnessing the gulags and the tragedies of the Third or the Fourth worlds, recognise Job's demands from his dunghill as our own lament, our own cry. This is the time of the shattering of being; exploding, lacerating imprecation has replaced the careful structured speech we knew before Hiroshima and Auschwitz: Elie Wiesel met Job on every road and every path in Europe;[13] for Rubenstein, a Jew at Auschwitz was less even than a heap of dung: 'Job had gone up in smoke, and his question with him.'[14] As Hans Ehrenberg says in his book *Hiob der Existentialist*, 'Our time was ripe for Job.'[15]

It is not surprising, then, that a return of the tragic should have been paralleled by a return of Job. We have recently shown the extent of this return of Job in a study deliberately confined to the theatre in France. But the phenomenon is ubiquitous: Job is to be found today in painting, in the novel, on television, and in philosophic essays. To stay with the theatre, however, one of the most important events of the immediate post-war years was the production in 1947 of Kafka's *The Trial* adapted for the stage by Gide, who had the chaplain speak Job's own words, 'Are you condemning me so that you may be justified?', although these words do not appear in the original novel. As for Antonin Artaud, all post-war theatre is indebted to him for his esthetic of *cruelty*, so reminiscent of Job's frenzy. It would have been surprising therefore if Artaud, that victim personified, had never mentioned Job, and indeed he does so, in connection with the theatre, as one would expect: 'See the Book of Job.'[16] Ionesco, in *Notes et Contre-Notes*, deliberately takes Job as his patron. Job's name does not appear in the plays, but the situations often resemble his, and though Ionesco's exile never knows the joy of salvation or of escape from his predicament, Ionesco nonetheless affirms that he 'feels he is Job', and has not gone beyond the basic question: 'What is wanted of me?'[17] The work of Beckett, whom Ionesco defines as a contemporary of Job, is for its part even more steeped in Joban dereliction. Many critics have compared individual plays with the biblical book: the characters are all abandoned, seem to break up, and are 'dropped' by God.[18] In Billetdoux's *Comment va le monde, Môssieu?*, one of the two wanderers is named Job. Obaldia describes the stylite Oscar in *Et à la fin était le bang* as a Job perched on his dunghill.[19] Vauthier's combattant character, Antonine Maillet's

'Sagouine', the old folk in Arrabal's *Guernica*, Zénobie in Boris Vian's *Les Bâtisseurs d'empire*, and the master in Dubillard's *La Maison d'os* do not mention Job by name, but their faces wincing with pain or with their sorry smiles are like the grieving face of Job, whose grief is thus transformed into 'glory' and becomes an 'icon', i.e., longing for the Absent One. Recently, in *Apocalypsis cum figuris*, Grotowski put into the mouth of Lazarus the words of Job cursing the day he was born, and even more recently, in the 1978-79 season, the Rideau de Bruxelles staged the Book of Job itself. How 'modern' then is the face that, like a haunting metaphor, keeps appearing today, fleetingly but with force, in poems, novels and essays. It is the face of the suffering servant of Isaiah, the face of the buffeted Christ, the face of a sad clown like Charlie Chaplin or the tramps in *En attendant Godot*. Job, that nervous flotsam of our time, has something of them all. Countless writers today refer to him as they would to a quintessential figure: Cioran, an exacerbated Job; Benjamin Fondane, a follower of Chestov; Olivier Clément, of Dostoievsky; Gabriel Marcel ('I keep myself a pure centre of demand in the face of an absurd and brutal world'); Philippe Némo, the author of *Job et le'excès du mal*; Elie Wiesel; André Neher. . . . All these have described the Joban dark night of Trial, the 'montage de misère' Raymond Ruyer defines in *La Gnose de Princeton*, the anguish of being caught in a rational impasse one can see no escape from, the blindness induced in conscience by inability to give meaning to apparently arbitrary suffering, and the agonising question the contemporary German playwright Wolfgang Borchert writes as a cry of supplication and uses to close his so Joban play *Draussen vor der Tür*: 'Why are you silent? Why? Will no one answer?' 'Will no one listen to what I am saying?' (Job 31:35).

Because space was limited this article has concentrated on the presence and 'pregnancy' of Job in French literature. But in an age of cultural interchange, it should not be forgotten that the figure of Job is being both transmitted and received by every country in Europe. This is especially true of Germany, where Job can be found in the thirteenth century Hartmann von Aue's *Le Pauvre Heinrich*, in Heine's *Romancero*, and more recently in Ernst Bloch's Marxist reflections in *Atheismus in Christentum* and Ernst Jung's *Réponse à Job*. In our own day, against a backdrop of the death of God and the philosophy of the absurd, the suffering of the just is the object of reflection to which events we need not dwell on have given bitter depth. Many contemporary German writers are haunted by the distress of Job on his dunghill: Kokoschka's expressionist *Job* (1917) foreshadowed Joseph Roth's *Hiob: Der Roman eines einfachen Mannes* (1930), Karl Wolfskehl's book of poems *Job et les quatre miroirs* and Margarete Susman's *Das Buch Hiob und das Schicksal des Jüdischen Volkes* (1946).

Job has been and is a fertile source of inspiration in literature. The full extent of the phenomenon still needs to be explored, but it is such today that one has to ask whether Job is not acquiring the status of a myth, like Prometheus or Sisyphus. However, our work suggests rather that as a figure, Job has a compelling force that will prevent him solidifying into myth. He does not belong to fable, but is a figure of our human story as men, and for our part we prefer to speak of him in terms of 'presence'; he is a being which we cannot but perceive as representative and in whom we discover our identity. The retreat of the Divine, the eclipse of God leave an emptiness down which Job's words go echoing endlessly. And the Joban words are our words also: 'The air is full of our cries.'[20]

Translated by Ruth Murphy

Notes

Unless otherwise stated, place of publication is Paris.

1. R. Lebègue *La Tragédie religieuse en France* (Champion 1929).

2. T. Kantor *Le Théâtre de la mort* textes réunis par Denis Bablet (L'âge d'homme 1977).

3. See Voltaire *Histoire des voyages de Scarmentado* in *Romanes et contes* (Garnier). In Spanish, the *escarmentado* is someone who has been tested by experience to the point of bodily suffering.

4. Letter from Frederick II to Voltaire (Pléiade, Bestermann, 7554).

5. Lautréamont *Chants de Maldoror* chant 2 strophe 3.

6. Kierkegaard *Quatre discours édifiants* (Aubier 1843).

7. R. Reichelberg *L'Exil dans le théâtre et l'œuvre exégétique de Claudel* (Nizet 1976) p. 216.

8. G. Bernanos *Correspondance*, May 1983 (about *Monsieur Ouine*) quoted in A. Beguin *Bernanos par lui-même* (Seuil) p. 167.

9. G. Bernanos *La Joie* (Pléiade) p. 605.

10. Guy Suares *Malraux, celui qui vient* (Stock-Plus 1974) p. 28.

11. M. Friedmann *Problematic Rebel, An Image of Modern Man* (New York 1963). The author sees Dr Rieux as a modern Job (p. 436).

12. J. Green *Mille chemins ouverts* (Livre de poche) pp. 190-191.

13. E. Wiesel *Célébration biblique* (Job ou le silence révolutionnaire) (Seuil 1975) p. 196.

14. R. L. Rubenstein *L'Imagination religieuse* (NRF 1968) p. 54.

15. 'Unsere Zeit ist Hiob-reif geworden' 1952 (quoted in *AUMLA* 2 1954, H. MacLean 'The Job Drama in modern Germany').

16. A. Artaud *Œuvres complètes* (NRF) XI, p. 207.

17. E. Ionesco *Un Homme en question* (NRF 1979) p. 12.

18. See particularly the article by O. De Magny 'Samuel Beckett ou Job abandonné' *Monde nouveau-Paru* (No. 97, February 1956) p. 95.

19. R. De Obaldia *Œuvres complètes* VI, pp. 101-102.

20. S. Beckett *En attendant Godot* (ed. de Minuit) p. 128.

Conclusion

Christian Duquoc

Demonism and the Unexpectedness of God

'DEMONISM' IS a violent term, used for its shock effect. Nevertheless, in addition to the literary or journalistic effect of its symbolic power, the term has philosophical connotations, deriving from Ernst Bloch's *Atheism in Christianity*. Bloch, a heterodox Marxist, undertook to prove that 'only a Christian can be a good atheist'. The remark has a whiff of scandal, and in his book Bloch attempts to justify the paradox. To this end he constructs the following thesis. Two contradictory trends run through the Bible; one, referring to the God who created the world, belongs to a perspective dominated by the arbitrariness of power. The other, stemming from the work of Moses, the exodus, develops into the idea of a moral God fighting against injustices and mobilising his energy to give the poor a land. The preaching of the prophets has its foundation in this idea of a God who comes to establish a bright future. Ernst Bloch judges the two representations of God to be incompatible: the arbitrary power of creation cannot be reconciled with the revolutionary violence of the God of the exodus. One must supplant the other: the moral God of the prophetic preaching belonging to the exodus tradition cannot be the God conceived of as creator in terms of the domination of the masters. According to Bloch, the author of the Book of Job gives dramatic form to the battle between these two representations, but does not dare to draw the consequences. Only Jesus will have the courage to do this by substituting for God the son of man, that is, man. Jesus thus gives an atheist orientation to the Bible; he eliminates God's arbitrariness, his 'demonism'. And he banishes it because God cannot be justly imagined in any other way than as a moral idea. For my part, while noting the perspective opened up by Bloch, I should like to show in this article that 'demonism' is not necessarily arbitrariness, but the way in which human beings can avoid reducing God to a moral or reasonable idea. The first part of the article will discuss the question in relation to the Book of Job, the second in relation to the question raised by the cross of Jesus. The conclusion will refer to the impossibility of pinning God down and argue that this indicates his freedom and gratuitousness.

1. THE THEOLOGICAL DEBATE OF THE BOOK OF JOB

I shall not go into the exegetical problems raised by the book. I shall treat it as a dramatic poem which illustrates, in one sense, the dilemma into which the covenant plunged the people.

I mean the covenant. Inseparable from the ideas of election and promise, it had imprinted on the minds of the Jewish people the sense of having a guarantee against accidents. History, in this view, is guided by God in such a way that the chosen people acquire all they need for collective and individual happiness. The conviction, rooted in the people, that God was working for their benefit, was constantly battered by the experience of a distortion between human actions and their results. It was difficult to imagine any equivalence between the real value of actions and the guarantee for the future.

This sense of a distortion took on increasingly radical forms as the return from exile, proclaimed in such elevated imagery by the prophets, had been banal and Israel exhausted the energy supplied by the covenant in an ever more punctilious refinement of worship and the law. In my view the Book of Job's silence about the covenant is not designed to universalise a debate about innocent suffering, but to show that what had been thought of as Israel's privileged position does nothing to shield it from the most radical questions. An attempt to cover up the scandal of innocent suffering which breaks through on all sides by theories seeking to show the continuing justice of the covenant in Israel would be to delude oneself and ultimately not to do homage to God. The Book of Job therefore apparently abstracts from the covenant only to establish the most blatant scandal at its very centre. Job's friends are representatives of ideas current in Israel, ideas whose thrust seems to be the following: the God of Israel is a moral God, and all his activity in relation to human beings is based on a justice operating in ordinary history. Job does not accept the totalitarianism of this schema; he rejects the equation of his history and the justice of God. The author puts into God's mouth a speech which separates him from the equation between divine action in history and morality. No reply is given. The distortion is accepted: God cannot be defined in his action solely by the logic of the covenant.

This idea of a shift in God, indicated both by Job's revolt and the poetic language of God's speech (Job 38-42), has good biblical precedents. Ernst Bloch has taken the point that the ancient traditions describe episodes in which God's behaviour is unpredictable. Bloch refers to Gen. 2:5-3:24, which records God's ambiguous attitude towards human beings, Gen. 32:22-33, the story of Jacob's strange fight with the angel of God, who does not refuse to bless him but will not reveal his name, the episode of the tower of Babel (Gen. 2:1-9), which he interprets as God's impatience with human progress, Deut. 34, the account of the death of Moses on the threshold of the promised land. Bloch appeals to other texts to confirm the idea of the unexpectedness of God, such as the reversal of attitude between the account of the murder of Abel (Gen. 4:1-17) and the story of the sacrifice of Isaac (Gen. 22:1-20). Many other episodes, especially in the historical books, bear witness to the unexpected nature of divine action; references to the morality deriving from the covenant are inadequate to explain God's behaviour. Ernst Bloch gives the name 'demonism' to this unexpected quality of God, describing it as arbitrary power, in comparison with a moral proclamation seeking human liberation. Bloch says that God escapes our grasp in his action because that action does not fall within the framework of legality and morality postulated by the covenant and required by God's Mosaic name, 'I am who I shall be' (Exod. 3:14).

To talk of archaisms is not good enough here. One of the strengths of the author of Job, a late writer, is that he has made the archaisms relevant, while presenting them artistically as archaisms: Job is a figure from antiquity. Job's drama, however, reveals Israel's present contradiction: wanting a God who guides history according to a programme which is accessible through the three categories that govern the structure of the chosen people, election, covenant and promise. Forcing people to recognise that things are not like this leads to a double correction, giving a voice to the people and taking the ancient narratives seriously.

Giving a voice to the people. The prophets speak in the name of God. They take up a position over against the people and remind them of the demands of the covenant and the serious consequences of their transgression. They listen to the people only in order to refute their arguments. No doubt they make a selection among the people; they do not talk in the same way to the powerful and to the exploited. To the former they present an accusation; to the latter they bring a message of hope. But the comforting truth of their words always lies in the future; all that is verifiable is the misfortune. Israel is invaded, Israel is in exile, Israel is no longer politically independent. True, a Messiah, a king such as Yahweh desires, will arise, but he is not present. All that is effective is misfortune or accusation. And as for the fate of the individual, the prophets, so fascinated by their vision of history, are hardly interested.

The author of the Book of Job does not put anything on to anyone. He does not accuse; he listens to the growing complaints, grumbles, revolt. He measures the despair which has become an everyday phenomenon, because he knows the power of exploitation, the force of sickness and death. He does not describe a future in a land where milk and honey flow; experience has shown that these are only beautiful images people conjure up for each other in their tents in the desert to drive away the thought of hunger. The author of the Book of Job knows what people think, what people say in whispers—and not just in Israel. He measures, by experience, the vanity of explanatory theories like those offered by Job's friends and, perhaps behind them, the excessive optimism of the prophetic visions. He is wary of abstractions, the people, history, the covenant. He is a man of flesh: it is the fate of the individual which concerns him.

The opportunity to speak given here to the people does not detach them from God, but leads them to reflect that the God of Israel may not be wholly contained within the prophets' moral message. The history to which they constantly appeal to substantiate their accusations is not the only place in which God makes himself known. And even in history, does he make himself known as clearly as the prophets' sermons imply? Job doubts it. In this sense, the Book of Job gives new vigour to old traditions: God escapes from our calculations.

Restoring relevance to ancient narratives. The Bible is the result of a process of taming. In the time of Ezra and Nehemiah (450-400 b.c.), the priestly groups, often influenced by the prophetic message which had declared the covenant betrayed, made a selection among the traditions. The work of editing included a certain tidying up, and the voice of the people became less prominent in the new versions than the story deriving from the prophetic response to the historical failure of the covenant. The author of the Book of Job, by placing his theological debate outside the period of the rewriting and outside the sacred space of biblical territory, was able to make himself the echo of the idea taking shape in the ambiguous stories which the priestly tidiers were trying to purge. The idea which was taking shape was that God's action is not as transparent as implied by the prophetic message and dominant opinion. Through the apparently idolatrous attitude of the people in their attempts to get guarantees of divine favour, there emerges the conviction that the divine is not clear in its intentions. Many episodes in the crossing of the desert bear witness to this doubt about the intentions of God. In official teaching this counts as sin, because the leaders know what God wants. There was nothing to prove that things worked like this in the traditions in which the unexpectedness of God's action in relation to the ethical norms of the prophetic tradition became blatant. Job takes account of this 'irrationality'; it is not just in the order of morality that God's greatness must be conceived, but in the poetic play illustrated by the speech put into God's mouth. The elusiveness of God derives not primarily from the moral domain, but from that gratuitousness in action symbolised so remarkably by the profusion, the waste and the irrationality of the universe. This gratuitousness is a provocation when it cuts across an individual history; Job experiences this.

Between Job's experience and the unexpectedness of God there is a complicity, but only revolt could reveal it. This, it seems to me, is the paradox of the book; fidelity to the law misses the ambiguous gratuity of divine action. The revolt of Job, that attentive student of the world, makes him ready to listen to an account less reasonable than that purveyed by the language dominant at the time, a language claiming to honour the demands of the covenant and yet constantly refuted by events.

Complicity between Job's revolt and God's unexpectedness, then, is one of the meanings of the book. The complicity produces a paradoxical effect: impatient Job is restored to prosperity, while God's allies are rejected. The dramatic parenthesis is closed, but it was sufficiently expressive to establish the fragility of the covenant when attempts are made to transform it into a moral logic. The author establishes this radically. Job encounters God at the end of his revolt, and God recognises Job as the unpredictable element of the creation whose virtues he has spread out to view. Job is the most gratuitous of his creatures, the one whose friendship is the most prized. The only solution offered to the argument about innocent suffering is God's recognition of the right to revolt. But does not the cross of Jesus refute this interpretation?

2. THE UNEXPECTEDNESS OF THE CROSS

In the Book of Job the 'arbitrariness' of God is allied with Job's revolt. The gratuitousness of his action, the irrationality of his decisions, are more favourable to the suffering innocent than the judicial logic which the 'friends' find in the covenant. The same situation will be repeated many times in the Gospel: the defenders of the law and of the status of the covenant oppose Jesus. Jesus acts on a logic which appears to them incompatible with the seriousness demanded by the greatness of the link between Israel and God. It is not worthy either of a prophet or of a rabbi to break the sabbath to relieve distress which could be relieved on the morrow. It is not fitting that a person should proclaim his association with public sinners. It is disturbing that a devotee of the Mosaic law should claim the right to flout the law. Jesus' actions are judged to be arbitrary because his reference is not seen. The parables he tells, such as that of the workers hired at the eleventh hour, ridicule the social order; or, like that of the prodigal son, show contempt for the honest worker. They underline the incoherent features of his attitude, his proclamation of the reign of God without insisting on a clear order with a structure based on the law. Jesus' words and actions seem to have no logical basis. One sign of this is that propensity of his to contrast his 'I' with the remembered collective wisdom: 'It was said, but I say. . . .' In this way the gratuitousness inherent in God's speech about the creation finds an analogy in the gratuitousness underlying Jesus' actions. In the former case it becomes an accomplice of the innocent Job whose suffering makes a mockery of judicial logic; in the latter it takes its reference from those whom legal and religious society regard as rubbish. In both cases it is neither social logic nor moral logic which prevail, but a liberty which appears arbitrary and which yet forms an alliance with those whom morality and politics exclude. The cross of Jesus takes this common feature to an extreme.

The cross does not fit into any order; it is the result of an excessive Pharisaic passion for order. Jesus pays with his life for not having urged people to follow the law; he is eliminated because he denounced specific instances of its perverse effects. His appeal to conversion was rooted in a dimension, the cry of the desperate, which required an interpretation of the law different from the interpretation dominant at the time. Jesus' actions arise out of the rules imposed by a legal and social order which closes its eyes to their effects; Jesus highlights them, for no reason, just as Job, by his innocence, highlights the murderous logic of the 'friends'' interpretation. In Jesus' case the logic turns into the operation and justice of the law: he is sentenced and killed. The irrationality of the cross is swallowed up in the greater reason of the zealots for the law. No more than Job is Jesus a libertarian or an anarchist, but he does not hide the distortion between present oppression and the pretensions of the leaders. Job screamed this distortion to the heavens—he accused God of taking no notice of him—but the God he accused was the figure created by the 'friends', a God whose job was to watch over the equitable distribution of rewards and punishments. The reply is unexpected: God, in a different order, speaks a language analogous to Job's. The cosmos is not based on a moral law or a logic of equality; it is the realm of gratuitousness because it is 'play'. This God whose language is full of humour allies himself with Job the rebel against the 'friends' who think they understand his designs.

Jesus stresses the distortions; he opposes the leaders. He does not accuse God; he acts as if God were on his side. The leaders, however, lack the sense of humour of the God attacked by Job; they refuse to ratify Jesus' subversive statements. Order is reasonable, is right, and order kills Jesus, while God's arbitrariness, in the Book of Job, restores Job to life. God gives Jesus his life back after he has risen against logic because of its perverse effects.

Thus, if we give the name 'demonism' to the elusive aspect of divine activity, the impossibility of reducing it to a rule, we must recognise that God's action in the Book of Job forms the context for God's action in the drama of the cross. The outcast Jesus and the outcast Job are right because they have not allowed themselves to be imprisoned in the logic of morality. We can apply to the fate of Jesus, who rose to life through the Spirit, the conviction expressed by Job:

> I know for my part that my Redeemer lives,
> that he will rise up as the last on the dust.
> And after my skin has been thus destroyed,
> I shall still behold God in my flesh.
> I myself shall behold him!
> My eyes shall see him, and he will not be distant.
> My heart burns within me.
>
> [Job 19:25-27]

In a recent book a French writer, G. Morel, has simultaneously offered a defence of God and criticised Christian utilitarianism. Influenced by his studies of Nietzsche (*Nietzsche*, 3 vols., Paris 1971), he has pleaded for the reintroduction of 'play' and 'gratuitousness' into the realm of the divine. Quoting a verse of the German mystic Angelus Silesius,

> The rose has no reason. It flowers because it flowers; it pays no attention to itself and does not ask if it is seen.

he argues that God should no longer be imprisoned in the petty calculations imposed on him by Christianity's moral and anthropocentric interests. Without using the term 'demonism', he illustrates its meaning (G. Morel *Questions d'homme*, Paris 1977). Morel is suspicious to the point of obsessiveness of prophetic schemas conditioned by moral norms. It is not that he is a libertarian or an anarchist; he simply refuses to allow the relation to God to be applied to anything but its own plenitude. He rejects the functional use made of God's authority or of his immersion in our history. This God, emerging into our view from pure gratuitousness, is nevertheless different from the God against whom Job revolts; he is silent. Job calls on God to defend him, and so to reply to the accusation Job brings against him. God replies with the profusion of his speech symbolising the profusion of his creative acts and celebrating the illogical play of his works. His words make him an accessory to Job's demands although Job is still to some extent a prisoner of his 'friends'' theories, and he subordinates the word of God to justice before learning that justice is not the last word. He recognises this because God's action is 'uncalculating', a word of which Morel is fond. The 'uncalculating' nature of God is, however, something Job learns from God, not from reflection on experience which leads him to revolt. It is because there is 'no reason' to God's activity, any more than there is to the flowering of the rose, that it coincides with Job's demand to be allowed to escape from an order which is logical but absurd. Thus the Book of Job does not support Ernst Bloch's thesis that 'demonism' must be eliminated in favour of the secular ideal of the moral God; in unforgettable poems it argues that the calculating world of the scribes and judges is not that of the God revealed to Moses, and that the very intuitions of the prophets on control of history are in danger of blocking our access to God. Thus the same reproach stands against both the defenders of God's arbitrariness who are unable to entertain the plea of the innocent and oppressed and the idolators of just legality for whom gratuitousness, play and fantasy are qualities too trivial to clothe the deity in. The God of the Mosaic tradition is the defender of the oppressed precisely because he is not the regulator of order. Revolt, rising up from a heart and directed at him, is more to his liking than the invocation of his power to ensure the policing of the world. Jesus belongs to this camp; when he pardons the adulterous woman and rejects the application of the legal penalty, it is because that penalty closes off any future, and because the law, to its defenders, is more important than the woman. He pardons his killers because their future concerns him more than maintaining the balance between good and evil by means of a just distribution of misfortune. If he is more interested in the prodigal squandering his fortune than in the elder son making the family wealth increase, it is because the elder son has taken his own steps to give himself assets to protect him against the future, whereas the prodigal, having lost everything, has no other future than that awarded him by his potential judge, the Father. The elder son prefers order, the Father hope. The Book of Job is a blow against the moral desire to make use of God's power to realise one's own projects. If God's speech in the book is 'amoral', it is because in the context only this amorality was able to hear the plea of the oppressed.

It would be a pity if we were to deduce from the cross that the debate begun in the Book of Job is now redundant, that it has been left to us as a monument to a moment gone for ever, and that the figure of Job speaks to us now only through his patience in suffering. Nothing of the sort is true, in my view. The debate remains relevant—all the more so because the opposite temptations of a God who plays and dances (Nietzsche) and of a God identified with the secular moral order, are still with us. The God of Job plays at creation, but his play is not contempt, but freedom: he sits sufficiently loose to morals and programmes, history and liturgy, to take sides with the person who no longer has a house in the city, the excluded.[1] His play is not based on a legal justice or on judicial error; the order of things and historical progress matter little to God if they have to be paid for by the suffering of the innocent or built on the despair of a minority. God is more honoured by the impatience and revolt of Job than by the adulation of the 'friends' who recognise the designs of providence where God himself says he sees no such thing.

Translated by Francis McDonagh

Note

1. The thesis put forward here does not have a political intent: it seeks to show from biblical data that Job's revolt and the cross of Jesus mark the limit of all order and all politics. It implies that the person excluded does not enjoy absolute privilege, since exclusion may cover many things. The situations of the excluded innocent and of those who exclude themselves by crime are not the same. The abolition of the supremacy of order by pardon is not weakness, nor is it laxity or demagogy. Jesus does not condemn the adulterous woman, but he does not approve her conduct because he calls on her to be converted. Pardon presupposes that crime is called by its name. An immediate transposition of the Gospel into politics and law betrays the Gospel by running the risk of reducing it to an attitude which accepts everything from incapacity to resist anything or through bad conscience. Only the victim can genuinely pardon the killer. The Gospel does not suppress law; it places it in a different context. It is not an invitation to naiveté, but to lucid kindness. If it is not, it becomes an ideology made irresponsible by sentimentality.

Contributors

LUIS ALONSO-SCHÖKEL is professor of Biblical Introduction and Old Testament Theology in the Pontifical Biblical Institute in Rome, where he was Dean from 1975 to 1981. His publications include works on both Spanish and Hebrew poetry, and commentaries on the Prophets and Psalms.

MARC BOCHET was born in Paris in 1929. He holds university qualifications in philosophy, Spanish and French, including a Sorbonne doctorate on Job in post-war French drama. He has taught in Spain, Poland and Portugal and currently teaches at the European School in Brussels, Belgium.

FRANÇOIS CHIRPAZ teaches philosophy at the University of Lyons. He is an agrégé and a Docteur ès Lettres. His works include *Le Corps, Enjeux de la violence* (a study of René Girard), and *Difficile rencontre*. He is shortly to publish a study of Rousseau called *L'Homme dans son histoire*, and also *Hume et la procès de la métaphysique*.

JEAN COLLET has been film critic of the review *Etudes* since 1966. He lectures on the cinema and communication theory at the Universities of Paris 7 and Dijon, and is an adviser on the syllabus at the Institut National de l'Audio-visuel, Paris. As well as numerous articles he has published books on *Jean-Luc Godard* (1963 and 1972), *Le Cinéma en question* (1972) and *Le Cinéma de François Truffaut* (1977).

CHRISTIAN DUQUOC, OP, was born in Nantes (France) in 1926 and ordained priest in 1953. He holds a doctorate in theology and a diploma from the Ecole Biblique in Jerusalem. He teaches dogmatic theology in the theology faculty of the University of Lyon and is a member of the editorial board of the review *Lumière et Vie*. Fr Duquoc's publications include *Christologie*, 2 vols. (1972), *Jésus, homme libre* (1973) and *Dieu différent* (1977).

ENRIQUE DUSSEL was born in Argentina in 1934. He holds doctorates in philosophy from Madrid, history from the Sorbonne and theology from Fribourg, and teaches ethics in the National University of Mexico. He is President of the Latin American Study Commission on Church History, which is going to hold its first General Conference in autumn 1984. His recent published works include *Ethics and Theology of Liberation* (1978), *History of the Church in Latin America, 1492-1979* (1981) and *Philosophy of Liberation* (1983).

DIRK KINET was born in 1941 in Antwerp. He studied theology in Louvain and also in Tübingen, where he took his doctorate in 1976. Since 1971 he has taught biblical and oriental languages in the faculty of Catholic theology at the University of Augsburg. His publications include *Ba'al und Jahwe. Ein Beitrag zur Theologie des Hoseabuches* (Frankfurt 1977), *Ugarit—Geschichte und Kultur einer Stadt in der Umwelt des Alten Testamentes*, Stuttgarter Bibelstudien 104 (Stuttgart 1981) and *Bibelauslegung für die Praxis*, vol. 14: *Der aufhaltbare Untergang (Hosea, Joel, Amos, Micha)* (Stuttgart 1981). He has also contributed to *Bibel und Kirche, Biblische Zeitschrift* and *Freiburger Rundbrief*.

JEAN LÉVÊQUE, OCarm, was born in Soissons, Frânce (1930), and was ordained priest in the Carmelite Order (1959). He studied at Lille and subsequently at the Institut Orientaliste, Louvain, where he was awarded a doctorate in theology (1968). He is the author of *Job et son Dieu. Essai d'exégèse et de théologie biblique* (Paris 1970); he has also written several articles for journals of exegesis and spirituality. Since 1974 he has been professor of Old Testament exegesis and semitic languages at the Institut Catholique, Paris.

RODERICK MACKENZIE, SJ, is a Canadian. Born in 1911, he joined the Society of Jesus in 1928. He has an SSD from the Pontifical Biblical Institute, and was Rector of the same 1963-69. He contributed to the section on Job to the *Jerome Biblical Commentary*. He is now emeritus professor of Old Testament at Regis College in Toronto.

PHILIPPE ROUILLARD, OSB, was born in Paris (1926) and studied at L'Athénée St-Anselme (Rome). A doctor of theology, he lectured in liturgy at the Theological Faculty of Lille and was editor of the review *La Maison-Dieu* for a period of four years. Since 1972 he has been lecturing in liturgy and sacramental theology at L'Athénée St-Anselme. He has contributed to many reviews and encyclopaedias. On the Liturgy for the Dead he has published 'Les Liturgies de la mort' (*Notitiae*, 1976) and 'The Liturgy of the Dead as a Rite of Passage' (*Concilium* 112 (1978)).

JEAN-CLAUDE SAGNE, OP, was born in 1936 at Tours, France. He did his theological studies at the Dominican house of studies at L'Arbresle and was ordained in 1963. Besides degrees in the arts and theology, he has a doctorate in religious psychology, and now teaches social and clinical psychology at the University of Lyon-II. His publications include *Péché, culpabilité, pénitence* (1971); *Conflit, changement, conversion* (1974); *Tes péchés ont été pardonnées* (1971); *Présence du renouveau charismatique*.

CLAUS WESTERMANN's publications include the following: *Biblischer Kommentar AT. Genesis 1-11*, I/1 (1974; 1976) *Biblischer Kommentar AT. Genesis 12-36*, I/2 (1981); *Biblischer Kommentar AT. Genesis 37-50*, I/3 (1982); *Isaiah 40-66* (1969); *Basic Forms of Prophetic Speech* (1967); *Elements of OT Theology* (1982); *Praise and Lament in the Psalms* (1981); *Der Aufbau des Buches Hiob* (1977); *Sprache und Struktur der Prophetie Deuterojesajas* (1981); *Blessing in the Bible and in the Life of the Church* (1978); *The Promises to the Fathers* (1974); *Creation* (1974); *What Does the OT Say About God?* (1979); *Forschung am AT. Gesammelte Studien*, Theol. Bücherei (Munich) with bibliography vol. 24 (I) (1964), vol. 55 (II) (1974).

CONCILIUM

1. **The Church as Institution.** Ed. Gregory Baum and Andrew Greeley. 0 8164 2575 2 168pp.
2. **Politics and Liturgy.** Ed. Herman Schmidt and David Power. 0 8164 2576 0 156pp.
3. **Jesus Christ and Human Freedom.** Ed. Edward Schillebeeckx and Bas van Iersel. 0 8164 2577 9 168pp.
4. **The Experience of Dying.** Ed. Norbert Greinacher and Alois Müller. 0 8164 2578 7 156pp.
5. **Theology of Joy.** Ed. Johannes Baptist Metz and Jean-Pierre Jossua. 0 8164 2579 5 164pp.
6. **The Mystical and Political Dimension of the Christian Faith.** Ed. Claude Geffré and Gustavo Guttierez. 0 8164 2580 9 168pp.
7. **The Future of the Religious Life.** Ed. Peter Huizing and William Bassett. 0 8164 2094 7 96pp.
8. **Christians and Jews.** Ed. Hans Küng and Walter Kasper. 0 8164 2095 5 96pp.
9. **Experience of the Spirit.** Ed. Peter Huizing and William Bassett. 0 8164 2096 3 144pp.
10. **Sexuality in Contemporary Catholicism.** Ed. Franz Bockle and Jacques Marie Pohier. 0 8164 2097 1 126pp.
11. **Ethnicity.** Ed. Andrew Greeley and Gregory Baum. 0 8164 2145 5 120pp.
12. **Liturgy and Cultural Religious Traditions.** Ed. Herman Schmidt and David Power. 0 8164 2146 2 120pp.
13. **A Personal God?** Ed. Edward Schillebeeckx and Bas van Iersel. 0 8164 2149 8 142pp.
14. **The Poor and the Church.** Ed. Norbert Greinacher and Alois Müller. 0 8164 2147 1 128pp.
15. **Christianity and Socialism.** Ed. Johannes Baptist Metz and Jean-Pierre Jossua. 0 8164 2148 X 144pp.
16. **The Churches of Africa: Future Prospects.** Ed. Claude Geffré and Bertrand Luneau. 0 8164 2150 1 128pp.
17. **Judgement in the Church.** Ed. William Bassett and Peter Huizing. 0 8164 2166 8 128pp.
18. **Why Did God Make Me?** Ed. Hans Küng and Jürgen Moltmann. 0 8164 2167 6 112pp.
19. **Charisms in the Church.** Ed. Christian Duquoc and Casiano Floristán. 0 8164 2168 4 128pp.
20. **Moral Formation and Christianity.** Ed. Franz Bockle and Jacques Marie Pohier. 0 8164 2169 2 120pp.
21. **Communication in the Church.** Ed. Gregory Baum and Andrew Greeley. 0 8164 2170 6 126pp.
22. **Liturgy and Human Passage.** Ed. David Power and Luis Maldonado. 0 8164 2608 2 136pp.
23. **Revelation and Experience.** Ed. Edward Schillebeeckx and Bas van Iersel. 0 8164 2609 0 134pp.
24. **Evangelization in the World Today.** Ed. Norbert Greinacher and Alois Müller. 0 8164 2610 4 136pp.

115. **Doing Theology in New Places.** Ed. Jean-Pierre Jossua and Johannes Baptist Metz. 0 8164 2611 2 120pp.
116. **Buddhism and Christianity.** Ed. Claude Geffré and Mariasusai Dhavamony. 0 8164 2612 0 136pp.
117. **The Finances of the Church.** Ed. William Bassett and Peter Huizing. 0 8164 2197 8 160pp.
118. **An Ecumenical Confession of Faith?** Ed. Hans Küng and Jürgen Moltmann. 0 8164 2198 6 136pp.
119. **Discernment of the Spirit and of Spirits.** Ed. Casiano Floristán and Christian Duquoc. 0 8164 2199 4 136pp.
120. **The Death Penalty and Torture.** Ed. Franz Bockle and Jacques Marie Pohier. 0 8164 2200 1 136pp.
121. **The Family in Crisis or in Transition.** Ed. Andrew Greely. 0 567 30001 3 128pp.
122. **Structures of Initiation in Crisis.** Ed. Luis Maldonado and David Power. 0 567 30002 1 128pp.
123. **Heaven.** Ed. Bas van Iersel and Edward Schillebeeckx. 0 567 30003 X 120pp.
124. **The Church and the Rights of Man.** Ed. Alois Müller and Norbert Greinacher. 0 567 30004 8 140pp.
125. **Christianity and the Bourgeoisie.** Ed. Johannes Baptist Metz. 0 567 30005 6 144pp.
126. **China as a Challenge to the Church.** Ed. Claude Geffré and Joseph Spae. 0 567 30006 4 136pp.
127. **The Roman Curia and the Communion of Churches.** Ed. Peter Huizing and Knut Walf. 0 567 30007 2 144pp.
128. **Conflicts about the Holy Spirit.** Ed. Hans Küng and Jürgen Moltmann. 0 567 30008 0 144pp.
129. **Models of Holiness.** Ed. Christian Duquoc and Casiano Floristán. 0 567 30009 9 128pp.
130. **The Dignity of the Despised of the Earth.** Ed. Jacques Marie Pohier and Dietmar Mieth. 0 567 30010 2 144pp.
131. **Work and Religion.** Ed. Gregory Baum. 0 567 30011 0 148pp.
132. **Symbol and Art in Worship.** Ed. Luis Maldonado and David Power. 0 567 30012 9 136pp.
133. **Right of the Community to a Priest.** Ed. Edward Schillebeeckx and Johannes Baptist Metz. 0 567 30013 7 148pp.
134. **Women in a Men's Church.** Ed. Virgil Elizondo and Norbert Greinacher. 0 567 30014 5 144pp.
135. **True and False Universality of Christianity.** Ed. Claude Geffré and Jean-Pierre Jossua. 0 567 30015 3 138pp.
136. **What is Religion? An Inquiry for Christian Theology.** Ed. Mircea Eliade and David Tracy. 0 567 30016 1 98pp.
137. **Electing our Own Bishops.** Ed. Peter Huizing and Knut Walf. 0 567 30017 X 112pp.

138. **Conflicting Ways of Interpreting the Bible.** Ed. Hans Küng and Jürgen Moltmann. 0 567 30018 8 112pp.
139. **Christian Obedience.** Ed. Casiano Floristán and Christian Duquoc. 0 567 30019 6 96pp.
140. **Christian Ethics and Economics: the North-South Conflict.** Ed. Dietmar Mieth and Jacques Marie Pohier. 0 567 30020 X 128pp.
141. **Neo-Conservatism: Social and Religious Phenomenon.** Ed. Gregory Baum and John Coleman. 0 567 30021 8.
142. **The Times of Celebration.** Ed. David Power and Mary Collins. 0 567 30022 6.
143. **God as Father.** Ed. Edward Schillebeeckx and Johannes Baptist Metz. 0 567 30023 4.
144. **Tensions Between the Churches of the First World and the Third World.** Ed. Virgil Elizondo and Norbert Greinacher. 0 567 30024 2.
145. **Nietzsche and Christianity.** Ed. Claude Geffré and Jean-Pierre Jossua. 0 567 30025 0.
146. **Where Does the Church Stand?** Ed. Giuseppe Alberigo. 0 567 30026 9.
147. **The Revised Code of Canon Law: a Missed Opportunity?** Ed. Peter Huizing and Knut Walf. 0 567 30027 7.
148. **Who Has the Say in the Church?** Ed. Hans Küng and Jürgen Moltmann. 0 567 30028 5.
149. **Francis of Assisi Today.** Ed. Casiano Floristán and Christian Duquoc. 0 567 30029 3.
150. **Christian Ethics: Uniformity, Universality, Pluralism.** Ed. Jacques Pohier and Dietmar Mieth. 0 567 30030 7.
151. **The Church and Racism.** Ed. Gregory Baum and John Coleman. 0 567 30031 5.
152. **Can we always celebrate the Eucharist?** Ed. Mary Collins and David Power. 0 567 30032 3.
153. **Jesus, Son of God?** Ed. Edward Schillebeeckx and Johannes-Baptist Metz. 0 567 30033 1.
154. **Religion and Churches in Eastern Europe.** Ed. Virgil Elizondo and Norbert Greinacher. 0 567 30034 X.
155. **'The Human', Criterion of Christian Existence?** Ed. Claude Geffré and Jean-Pierre Jossua. 0 567 30035 8.
156. **The Challenge of Psychology to Faith.** Ed. Steven Kepnes (Guest Editor) and David Tracy. 0 567 30036 6.
157. **May Church Ministers be Politicians?** Ed. Peter Huizing and Knut Walf. 0 567 30037 4.
158. **The Right to Dissent.** Ed. Hans Küng and Jürgen Moltmann. 0 567 30038 2.
159. **Learning to Pray.** Ed. Casiano Floristán and Christian Duquoc. 0 567 30039 0.
160. **Unemployment and the Right to Work.** Ed. Dietmar Mieth and Jacques Pohier. 0 567 30040 4.

All back issues are still in print and available for sale. Orders should be sent to the publishers,

T. & T. CLARK LIMITED
■ **36 George Street, Edinburgh EH2 2LQ, Scotland** ■

GOD IS NEW EACH MOMENT

Edward Schillebeeckx

IN CONVERSATION WITH
HUUB OOSTERHUIS & PIET HOOGEVEEN

In response to the probing questions of his colleagues,
Edward Schillebeeckx provides a fascinating and comprehensible overview of his intellectual development and the
concrete implications of the major themes in his work. **GOD
IS NEW EACH MOMENT** permits an encounter with the flesh-
and-blood Schillebeeckx – a man whose thinking is driven
by his passionate concern to live a gospel Christianity that
is engaged with the great social, political, and intellectual
issues of the modern world. Clearly distilled are his ideas
about Jesus, the Scriptures, ministry and sacraments, the
future of the Church, the feminist movement, the liberation
of the poor. **GOD IS NEW EACH MOMENT** explores the sources
of Schillebeeckx' thought: the people, ideas, and experiences that have shaped his work.
144 pages   published in paperback

in the United States & Canada   in the United Kingdom
⅂Ɛ SEABURY PRESS   T. & T. Clark, Ltd.
Seabury Service Center · Somers, CT 06071

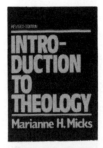

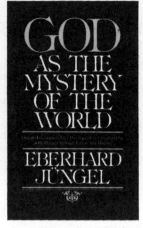
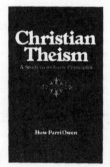

Note

Concilium 170, December 1983
THE MOVEMENT OF THEOLOGY SINCE THE COUNCIL
edited by E. Schillebeeckx, P. Brand, A. Weiler

This issue will be looking at the past, present and future of
Concilium, its place amid other post-Vatican II theological
trends and will give details of the new-look 1984 *Concilium*.

ETHICS BETWEEN HUMAN AUTONOMY AND
CHRISTIAN LIBERATION
will now be the subject of the April 1984 issue.